M

DEC

THE NEW

MORTGAGE MARKET

DECODING
THE NEW
MORTGAGE MARKET

Insider Secrets for
Getting the Best Loan
Without Getting Ripped Off

David Reed

AMACOM

American Management Association

New York • Atlanta • Brussels • Chicago • Mexico City • San Francisco
Shanghai • Tokyo • Toronto • Washington, D.C.

Special discounts on bulk quantities of AMACOM books are available to corporations, professional associations, and other organizations. For details, contact Special Sales Department, AMACOM, a division of American Management Association, 1601 Broadway, New York, NY 10019.
Tel: 800-250-5308. Fax: 518-891-2372.
E-mail: specialsls@amanet.org
Website: www.amacombooks.org/go/specialsales
To view all AMACOM titles go to: www.amacombooks.org

This publication is designed to provide accurate and authoritative information in regard to the subject matter covered. It is sold with the understanding that the publisher is not engaged in rendering legal, accounting, or other professional service. If legal advice or other expert assistance is required, the services of a competent professional person should be sought.

Library of Congress Cataloging-in-Publication Data

Reed, David (Carl David), 1957-
    Decoding the new mortgage market : insider secrets for getting the best loan without getting ripped off / David Reed.
      p.   cm.
    Includes index.
    ISBN-13: 978-0-8144-1400-2 (pbk.)
    ISBN-10: 0-8144-1400-1 (pbk.)
    1. Mortgage loans—United States.   2. Mortgage loans—Government policy—United States.   3. Secondary mortgage market—United States.   4. Housing—Finance—Government policy—United States.   I. Title.
    HG2040.5.U5R44   2010
    332.7'220973—dc22   2009033204

Printing number

10   9   8   7   6   5   4   3   2   1

Contents

What Happened, and How Did We Get Here?

TO THE CONSUMER, it may seem like a mortgage is a mortgage is a mortgage. Find a house, put some money down, and move in. But the mortgage industry has gone through some major changes that affect absolutely everyone who wants to obtain financing to buy a home. Everyone.

Understanding and interpreting these changes is critical to properly planning for the right financing. Make a mistake, and you'll get the wrong loan. A mistake on a 30-year mortgage means a potential reminder of that mistake for the next 360 months. It can even mean the difference between getting approved or not getting approved.

What used to be a complex mess of literally hundreds of different loan types has now been broken down into two basic categories: conventional and government. But those loans have also taken on their own twists and turns like never before.

For a 30-year fixed-rate loan, there are now literally 54 permutations to calculate not only the rate and terms but the literal approval itself. Loan programs have vanished. Credit guidelines have been restored to their original roots and in some cases made more onerous. Still others provide financing options not available before.

It used to be that simply applying for a mortgage loan meant an approval of some type, somewhere. No longer. It also used to mean that almost anyone could be in the mortgage business and become a "loan officer." No longer.

This is the first book that lays out the new rules, why they're there and how to get approved in the new mortgage market. Or perhaps "new" isn't the best descriptor. Perhaps it's simply a reversion to original lending guidelines. In reality, both statements are correct.

But to understand where we are now, we have to understand how we got here.

A LITTLE HISTORY

Early in the twentieth century, mortgages were made the old-fashioned way. When someone wanted to buy a home, the bank would have a meeting and decide whether to make a loan. If it decided its customer was deemed worthy of a home loan, it would go to the vault, or most likely write a check, on behalf of the borrower paid to the seller of the real estate. Needless to say, many people were kept out of home ownership in the metropolitan areas.

Even if you could get a mortgage, the terms made it such that only the rich people could get a home loan, as the down payment could be as high as 50 percent or more. One would think that if the down payment were 50 percent, then why even bother with getting a loan—why not keep saving for the down payment until there was enough money to write a check for the entire amount?

The loan would go to a loan committee and the participants would review things such as the customer's income and profession. They would review the customer's history with the bank to make sure the applicant had paid all previous loans on time.

If the bank felt good about the loan, voila, new homeowner.

As the country began to sink into the throes of the Great Depression in the late 1920s, pretty much everything financial came to an abrupt halt. The stock market crashed, home values declined, and people were laid off from their jobs.

Among other things, it took the government to help an economy mired in economic distress and fear. (Does anything sounding remotely familiar here?)

In 1934, the Federal Housing Administration was created under the auspices of the Department of Housing and Urban Development, and FHA loans were created. Actually, FHA loans aren't loans but are just called that. FHA instead insures mortgage loans. If a bank made a loan that conformed to FHA guidelines and the loan went into default, the lender would get its money back.

This loosened the purse strings of the bankers, and soon mortgage loans became a bit more commoditized with the introduction of FHA-insured mortgage loans. The plan worked, and more loans were being made to more people with less money down.

However, banks need to have money to loan money. If they ran out of money, they would have to advertise and raise more money through offering interest on people's deposits. If, for instance, they offered a savings account paying 2 percent, they could take enough money and charge someone getting a home loan 5 percent and make 3 percent off of the money. This is a bit simplistic, but at its core is exactly how it worked. Banks would lend the money they received from their depositors. It's also why banks worked more with wealthier people, because it was those people who had the assets that needed to be protected. At least that was the theory.

In practice, banks sometimes ran out of money to lend. Thus, the Federal National Mortgage Association (FNMA), or Fannie Mae, was created in 1938 to foster home ownership. It also operated under the auspices of HUD.

Fannie's job was to buy mortgage loans from banks that made FHA-insured mortgage loans when banks ran out of money to lend. This was the infancy of what is called the "secondary" *market* for mortgage loans, which we'll discuss in detail later in the chapter.

The federal government provided Fannie Mae with money, and Fannie Mae began to establish guidelines for the types of loans it would buy. If a loan conformed to these newly issued guidelines, Fannie would buy the loan from the issuing bank if the bank wanted to sell the loan and free up its capital to make more loans.

In 1944 as part of the GI Bill, zero-down mortgage loans were available for returning war veterans, and the pace of home buying began to pick up; the effects of the Great Depression were long since gone.

During this very brief period from 1934 to 1944, the mortgage industry began to show its force in the economy. When people bought their own homes, they also bought all the other stuff that went with home ownership, like furniture, appliances, and general maintenance on the home.

As more and more veterans returned from the war, lenders were making more loans than ever—both VA loans as well as FHA-insured ones. Banks began to lend like never before, and a housing boom went right along with the Baby Boom.

Things worked this way throughout the 1950s and 1960s. In 1968, Fannie broke away from HUD, and a couple of years later, the Federal Home Loan Mortgage Corporation (FHLMC), or Freddie Mac, was formed. In 1968, Fannie's charter changed to become a *government-sponsored entity,* or GSE.

Fannie was a private company that issued its own stock but was sponsored by the federal government. Although it wasn't exactly a business owned by the government, it was close to it. Freddie's chartering in 1970 was set up the same as Fannie Mae. Both entities were supposed to foster home ownership by freeing up cash for lenders in the mortgage markets.

But at the same time, both had stockholders they had to please. Fannie and Freddie both had an obligation from the federal government to provide liquidity in the mortgage marketplace, while at the very same time had to satisfy their shareholders to make a profit. The

GSE was an interesting experiment, crossing government and private enterprise with two separate goals.

Things went smoothly for much of the next 20 years. Then things began to change, slowly, for the worse.

SECONDARY MARKET GROWTH

Although the two GSEs went along buying mortgage loans from lenders, they did so by issuing their own underwriting guidelines, much the way FHA did. The GSEs didn't guarantee the loan in case it went bad but guaranteed that if the loan was underwritten to Fannie or Freddie standards, there would be someone to buy that loan.

One of those guidelines was the maximum loan limits set by Fannie and Freddie. As part of their lending guidelines, each would set their own loan limit each year. The problem was that there were other markets where houses were selling for much more than the conforming loan limits and buyers were saddled with going to a savings and loan and getting adjustable rate mortgages without the benefit of lower fixed rates offered with FHA and conforming loans.

A new secondary market was established for these loans that were above the conforming limits; they were nicknamed "jumbo" loans. Residential Funding Corporation, or RFC, was privately established to buy and sell jumbo mortgage loans with underwriting guidelines similar to conforming loans.

Other secondary markets were soon established to buy and sell mortgage loans that went beyond the standard conforming and government fare. Soon, capital markets were established that would facilitate buying and selling of other loans, such as loans that didn't document income or assets or loans made to those with bad credit.

If there wasn't a secondary market, mortgage bankers could invent a new type of mortgage loan and pitch it to some investors on Wall Street who could agree to buy these new mortgages if the bank made them.

The pitch might go like this: "We've got a new loan program here designed for those who can't quite prove their income, but we know its there. The advantage is that the returns on these investments provide an insured return of at least 11.15 percent," or some such. The secondary market provided the housing market with even more flex in its muscles. The mortgage market became a major player in finance around the world.

SUBPRIME LOANS

For 70 years, the mortgage market was, give or take, on autopilot. Loan guidelines rarely changed, as government and conventional loans all had to meet their respective rules. In the late 1990s, a couple of loan types began to emerge, and they weren't government or conventional. They were subprime and alternative. Subprime loans were so labeled because the credit grades of the borrowers were "less than prime." Alternative loans were sometimes called "Alternative A," or simply "Alt A" because even though the credit grade of the applicants was good, the loans didn't fit the conventional or government box. It was an alternative to conventional or government loans.

Subprime lenders have been around for 20 or so years and required that the borrowers have more money down for their purchase, usually a minimum of 20 percent or more.

Subprime loans, then, were designed for those who had enough money for a down payment but, for whatever reason, ran through some hard times. They were laid off from work or otherwise lost their main source of income. Perhaps there was a death in the family—such an event can wreak havoc on anyone's financial profile. When losing a loved one, it can be hard to concentrate on making the car payment on the first of the month.

Subprime loans were designed as a temporary solution to fix a mortgage problem. Their rates were much higher than what could be found for those with good credit, but were a temporary fix—a financial Band-Aid. The trick with subprime loans was to get someone into a house with a mortgage and begin to repair their credit with timely mortgage payments and meeting all other credit obligations each month, every month.

After a couple of years' worth of good credit behavior, the subprime borrower could then apply for a refinance mortgage into a traditional conventional or government loan. This typically worked because the borrowers had to pony up some major cash at the closing table, and the subprime loan provided a path to credit repair. Subprime loans weren't intended to be issued to those who had no intention of paying anyone back on time.

Alternative loans, or alt A loans, also had their intended market—those who couldn't or didn't care to divulge their income or asset information. Often times, this meant someone who was obviously very well-to-do, had good credit, and could perhaps have a very complicated financial portfolio.

I recall a client here in Austin who was wealthy, owned several corporations and investments, and hence some complicated tax returns. Alt A loans will accept "stated" applications, meaning the income or asset information isn't documented by tax returns or bank statements but instead relies on sufficient down payment and excellent credit. People with excellent credit didn't get excellent credit by accident: they earned it over a period of time.

My client's tax returns for all his businesses, and this wasn't even counting his assets, were literally eight inches thick. Alt A loans don't require all the typical documentation. In lieu of that documentation, the loans accept a sizable down payment and also a slightly higher interest rate. If a conventional jumbo loan could be found for 7.00 percent, then an alt A loan might be available for 7.25 percent. This is such a small increase in rate in exchange for fewer headaches.

In each case of subprime or alt A loans, lenders made sure there was a pool of buyers for those loans. They guaranteed significant rates of return, while at the same time churning out loans day after day and opening up credit markets that weren't previously available. But that presented a slight problem. If a lender came up with a mortgage loan that addressed a segment of the consumer market, what if the market soon became saturated and there was no longer any consumer to offer that loan to?

Subprime and alt A lenders would regroup, identify another market segment they could offer a new loan program to, and then pitch it to investors, who would buy those loans. After all, so far, the buyers of those loans were making tons of money.

In the early 2000s, subprime and alt A loans began to take charge of the mortgage lending environment in the United States. In fact, in many estimates, these loans managed to capture nearly 40 percent of all loans made in the country. Think about that for a second. Since the early 1900s, FHA, VA, Fannie, and Freddie, were the mortgage rule of law. Suddenly, and for a very short period, subprime and alt A loans collectively owned more of the mortgage market than Fannie, Freddie, VA, or FHA did individually.

This also came about when the federal government was making a major push for home ownership. Since owning a home was such a major force in the economy, not to mention the pride of home ownership, the government began to require banks to make loans to people who didn't necessarily qualify under traditional circumstances. Moreover, mortgage bankers—who simply find loans to make and then sell those loans—ultimately saw that they were running out of people and businesses to make loans to. If they didn't create new markets, they would be out of business.

So mortgage companies would go to a group of investors and say something to the effect of: "Okay, you guys made a ton of money with our new 10 percent down purchase with a 600 credit score, but we've got a new one for you that's just as profitable. How about 5 percent down and a 600 credit score?"

The investors would say, "Heck, yeah!" and provide a vehicle for those mortgage bankers to sell more loans. So they saturated the market for those with a 600 credit score and 5 percent down. What about 580 score and zero down? What about a 500 score and zero down?

More and more money kept flowing to the secondary markets, which kept buying more mortgages from subprime and alternative lenders. That's a lot of money, so where did the secondary markets get their money in the first place? They could package them up with millions of dollars' worth or more mortgages in securities, or bonds.

Instead of selling a $300,000 loan here and a $150,000 loan there, multiple loans were bundled together and sold as one large package to investors around the world. Wall Street got heavily involved in this so far profitable venture and began rolling not just mortgage loans together but all sorts of bonds. Wall Street also had bond-rating agencies give these mega-investments solid ratings so the buyers of these packages were assured of a top-tier performance with no delinquencies.

There was even something new called a "credit default swap" that provided those investors with an insurance policy that would pay them back their losses in case the bonds ever went bad or they lost their top rating due to loan defaults. The company who wrote those insurance policies was AIG. More money fueled more money, and investors were eager to buy more of these bond mortgage bonds. Mortgage companies were constantly challenged to find new markets.

As markets dwindled, the quality of loans had to deteriorate to accommodate the new loan programs being offered. Still, because loans had been performing and investors had been making so much money from these loans, they were willing to continue to provide funds.

Subprime and alternative lenders got their product in front of the consumer by concentrating heavily on mortgage brokers. Mortgage brokers could find these new clients and promote the new mortgages to their local communities.

Each time a new mortgage was invented, the mortgage companies sent out their notices to their mortgage brokers promoting the new product and who it was designed for.

Does your borrower have hard-to-prove income?
Does your borrower have no money down?
Does your borrower have a credit score of 520?
Then this is the mortgage for you!

Not only did the new loans find new customers, but it was an easy pitch for the loan officer: "David, I know the rates are higher, but this will give you time to repair your credit while still being able to write off the mortgage interest on your tax returns. In three years, your credit will be repaired, your property will have appreciated, and you can refinance into a conventional mortgage and avoid the higher rates!" was the standard presentation.

In addition to the easy sell of the mortgage itself, mortgage companies paid big bucks to the mortgage broker to sell the product, even if it meant the customer could have gotten a better deal by going FHA or conventional.

Mortgage brokers were getting as much as 4 percent additional on each mortgage loan they placed. On a $300,000 loan, that's another $12,000 lenders paid brokers to promote subprime and alternative loans. It's no stretch to understand why mortgage brokers began to promote these loans at the peril of the consumer: They were getting rich.

I recall a sad story about a couple just outside of Washington, D.C. I received an e-mail from an older gentleman about a loan he had taken out a year earlier. He had just received a notice from his lender that his loan payment was going to more than double, and he wouldn't be able to make the payments. What could he do?

I called him up on the phone and got a little more information about his loan and his situation. He was 75 years old, disabled, and had been so almost all of his life with a cognitive disorder. It takes him a long time to decipher things, and he even related to me that it took him about half an hour to compose his short five-sentence e-mail to me.

His wife was working at Wal-Mart to help supplement their income, and she was 65. They had bought the house they were living in about 12 years earlier and were about halfway through their mortgage. One day, pretty much out of the blue, they received a postcard, then a phone call, from a mortgage broker explaining how he could drop their monthly payments down to almost $1,100 from the nearly $1,700 they were paying each month.

Living on fixed incomes and working part time at Wal-Mart, the lower monthly payments looked attractive and seemed like a good way to save some money each month.

What the loan officer didn't explain was that, yes, while the monthly payments were lower by $600, it was what is called a "negative amortization" loan, explained in Chapter 6. This meant that each month they didn't pay another $900 every month, it would be added back onto their loan.

The mortgage actually grew in size instead of being paid down. Soon, the added amounts triggered a clause in their mortgage that made their payments nearly double after about only a year.

He wanted to know if there was anything he could do, and unfortunately, there wasn't. All of the proper disclosures that are designed to make people aware of such negative loan terms were signed by the borrowers—they simply didn't understand them. All they saw was their monthly payment was going to drop. They didn't know they would be in danger of losing the home they planned to live in for the rest of their lives.

The only thing they could do was sell the home or be foreclosed on. I sent them the name of a good real estate agent out of D.C., and they got together to check their options. Unfortunately, home values had declined so much that they owed more on the house than what it was currently worth. They would have had to come to the closing table with about $30,000. The real estate agent contacted the lender and began to negotiate a short sale (explained in Chapter 8), and the lender finally accepted after three months of effort.

The homeowners lost their home and their credit and moved into an apartment. All because some fast-talking mortgage broker talked them into a loan they had absolutely no business taking.

This true story was duplicated all across the country. Loan officers profited as alternative lending grew and grew.

FHA suffered. In fact, according to the GAO, FHA's market share dropped from 32 to 7 percent of the market share from 1996 to 2005. And it wasn't just FHA loans that were dwindling. So were conventional loans from Fannie and Freddie. Although FHA simply insures mortgages made by lenders, Fannie and Freddie had stockholders to satisfy. They decided to join the alternative and subprime party.

Both GSEs introduced loan programs designed for the subprime borrower to compete head-on with the subprime mortgage companies. They also invented various types of loans that didn't require pay stubs or tax returns, to compete with alternative lenders. Moreover, they bought into the notion that home prices will always appreciate, and if the borrowers ever got in trouble, they could always sell and get out from under the mortgage.

Home prices, on the whole, have always appreciated over time. Especially so during the mortgage loan heydays of the first half of the 2000s. Rates were low, and at the same time, home prices were still appreciating. This was all during the Iraq War, and one would think that through a pressing political climate an economy would be held in check. But not in the United States.

If homeowners ever got in trouble and fell behind in their mortgage payments the thinking was that they could always sell the property and come out ahead. In fact, many became real estate "investors" and bought real estate under relaxed credit guidelines, with the thinking that, "Hey, if worse comes to worse, I can always sell or refinance." Or maybe they can't, if home values don't appreciate. We'll discuss that ramification in detail in Chapter 8.

Around early 2007, something interesting (and problematic) began happening. Those people who took out subprime mortgage loans began to default on their mortgage. By itself, it seems nothing more than a late payment on a loan. But because these loans were ultimately packaged with other instruments in the form of megabonds, those defaults affected the performance of the bond itself.

At the same time, alternative loans began to become delinquent. And those same investments began to sour as well. Revenue streams that were expected from all these various transactions came to a halt. People began to default on their mortgages at breakneck speed.

The economy was in a slow down, home values began to deteriorate, and people couldn't refinance out of those mortgages. Home sales also slowed, and people couldn't sell their property and get out from under the mortgage. Hybrids and adjustable-rate mortgages began to reset at interest rates triple what they were before.

Now the investment lost its top-tier rating. Now the holders of those bonds were asking for money from those who sold the bonds to make up for their losses. AIG paid billions out to investors who purchased their credit default swap policies that protected them against loan defaults.

Almost everyone involved in the alternative and subprime business started to go broke. When a mortgage loan goes bad, the investor can send the loan back to the mortgage company and force a buyback of the loan. But mortgage bankers aren't equipped to buy back mortgages. They make their income on selling and servicing loans, not buying them back.

Mortgage brokers certainly can't buy back bad mortgages. They only get paid by finding a mortgage loan for a mortgage lender. Many of them also went out of business. The mortgage landscape had changed within a matter of months.

FALLOUT OF THE SUBPRIME COLLAPSE

Perhaps the most dramatic episode during all this mayhem was the near collapse of Fannie Mae and Freddie Mac. They had made too many bad loan decisions and made mortgages to people who couldn't afford them. The federal government took them over. You and I now own our own little slivers of Fannie and Freddie.

To stave off any future failures, the lenders that were still in business stopped making alternative and subprime loans almost immediately. Even if they wanted to make an alternative or subprime loan, they couldn't sell them because there weren't any buyers.

Many national banks and mortgage companies stopped doing business with mortgage brokers as well. We'll discuss mortgage bankers and mortgage brokers in detail in Chapter 5.

Mortgage brokers claimed they had a 50 to 60 percent market share in the United States. Some estimates were even higher, at nearly two-thirds of all loans originated by mortgage brokers. That number has fallen to as little as 10 percent of all mortgage loans in the country being originated by mortgage brokers.

Credit guidelines have tightened up as well, and for the first time, lenders now use a combination of credit scores and equity to help calculate an interest rate for a borrower. There are now required minimum credit scores for mortgage loans.

But it's not true that only those with perfect credit and 20 percent down can get a mortgage loan. Interestingly enough, those government stalwarts of VA, FHA, and now USDA remained unscathed during all that period. They stuck to their underwriting guidelines that have been used for decades. The same can now be said for both Fannie and Freddie. Yes, they tightened their credit guidelines, but in reality, what they did was go back to their original credit standards and they got out of the alternative and subprime business altogether.

There have been calls that the mortgage industry is unregulated and loose and there should be tighter restrictions on them. The notion that they're unregulated is not true. Having worked in the mortgage business as long as I have, I can tell you that plenty of laws are in place to regulate and monitor mortgage companies.

The problems occur when people don't follow the guidelines, cheat, or lie their way around them. Any mortgage loan that doesn't require documenting income or assets leaves itself open for fraud. And with the potential income an individual can make on a mortgage loan, it can be tempting for some with few morals to fudge this number or inflate that number.

Stated income loans were designed as a borrower convenience, not as a way to qualify people for mortgage loans that they would not be qualified for otherwise. But these loans were placed in the wrong hands, those that had the ability to defraud the system.

The mortgage companies who relied on alternative and subprime loans are out of business. The loans that regulators have decried simply don't exist any longer. So what does exist?

The core mortgage market now rests with conventional and government lending. We'll discuss both in detail in Chapters 2 and 3, but that's where the money is. I think it's ironic that we've ended up with what we started out with more than 70 years ago—but with important twists.

Although the staple loans are now Fannie, Freddie, VA, and FHA, they all now have their own set of guidelines and rules never seen before. Without knowing how these new rules piece together, one can get placed in the wrong mortgage program and pay for that mistake every month, or placed in an even worse situation: being declined for a mortgage loan in the new mortgage lending environment.

Fannie Mae and Freddie Mac: Underwriting Changes That Affect Every Potential Homeowner

WE MENTIONED BOTH Fannie Mae and Freddie Mac in the first chapter, but now let's take a closer look at how both operate, what their place is in the mortgage industry, and the new lending guidelines they issue.

When lenders make a loan, they do so for a profit. They charge an interest rate at which they'll get an annual return. For instance, if you borrowed $200,000 at 6 percent on a 30-year fixed-rate mortgage, the lender expects to get a rate of return of 6 percent on that loan. Easy enough.

Say, now, a lender makes not just one $200,000 loan but a hundred of them. The housing market is picking up steam, and the lender wants to make as many loans as possible to cash in on the home finance wave. That's a lot, but this explains how lenders operate on a daily basis. A hundred $200,000 loans is $20 million. Not many lenders have that kind of money lying around, but say in this example that this one does. The lender who lends $20 million might not be satisfied with "only" lending that amount and wants to lend more. But its vaults are empty. It ran out of money. So what does it do? The lender turns to the secondary market.

In the olden days, mortgage loans (in fact, all loans), were issued based on the amount of deposits a bank or savings and loan had in their vaults. Remember the movie *It's A Wonderful Life* when the Bailey Building and Loan experienced a bank run and the customers wanted all their money back? George told them they were thinking of the place all wrong. The money wasn't in the bank—it was in their neighbors' homes, who had borrowed their money to build and were paying it back. That's how banks made loans; they would attract depositors by offering them a return on their money and charging a higher interest rate when they loaned that same money back out to its customers.

That's no longer how it works with home loans. Enter the secondary market. Secondary markets are where mortgage loans are bought and sold between different banks, mortgage companies, and finally the mortgage giants Fannie Mae, Freddie Mac, and Ginnie Mae. Ginnie Mae is the acronym for the Government National Mortgage Association and it regulates government-backed VA and FHA loans. A lender can sell a loan to another lender at a discount, replenishing its mortgage coffers with new cash so it can continue to make more mortgage loans. How can lenders do this and make a profit?

If you take a standard 30-year fixed rate mortgage at 6 percent on a $200,000 loan, the lender would make over $230,000 in interest charges over the entire term of the loan. That's a lot of money. The problem with that scenario is that 30 years is a long time to recover $230,000. Maybe the lender can't or doesn't want to wait that long, so the lender sells the loan to a new lender, who will then collect the monthly interest as profit.

A typical loan sale might make $2,000 on a $200,000 transaction, surely much less than the $230,000 in unrealized interest, but the lender gets its money right away and gets its original $200,000 back to make more loans. Now multiply that amount by the 100 or so loans the lender might make every month, and that $200,000 single loan turns into 100 loans totaling $20 million. One percent of that is $200,000 in profit if all of those loans were sold.

Why would one bank want to sell loans while another bank wants to buy them? Don't all banks react the same way to current market conditions? Generally, but at the same time, a lender might have different investment strategies than another. One bank might want to aggressively enter a mortgage market and make lots of loans and sell or keep all, none, or some of them. Another bank may want to quietly sit back and collect a safe return of 6 percent each month and make money that way. Less risk, little to no overhead, and a planned rate of return over an extended period of time. Banks simply can have different strategies just as any other type of business can. Banks can buy and sell mortgages, mortgage lenders can buy and sell, and of course so can Fannie and Freddie.

The entities buy mortgages but buy lots of them, as in trillions of dollars' worth. When businesses sell mortgages to each other, ultimately one buyer is the last holder of the mortgage. No one else is buying. The mortgage itself could have been sold two, three, or four times over the course of a few years. When a bank has been buying mortgages over the years and suddenly wants to start making more home loans, it is caught in a predicament: Since it bought all those loans, it too is out of money to lend. So who does this last lender sell to? Fannie Mae, Freddie Mac, and Ginnie Mae.

These organizations were designed to provide the cash, or "liquidity" in the mortgage marketplace. If a bank wanted to sell its mortgages but no other lenders wanted to buy them, it would sell those loans to one of these three institutions. By providing this cash to banks, it creates the liquidity needed to make more home loans.

At first glance, it might seem to be an easy enough proposition to sell a mortgage from one lender to the next, but when loans are sold they aren't "approved" all over again. If you apply for a home loan and get approved and then your lender sells your mortgage, you don't have to go through the approval process all over again. How does the "buying" bank know what it is getting if it doesn't examine the loan application? The selling lender guarantees, or "warrants" that the loan it is selling conforms to a predetermined set of lending criteria established by Fannie Mae, Freddie Mac, and Ginnie Mae.

For instance, let's look at five different loans:

1. 30-year fixed on $200,000 at 6 percent
2. 25-year fixed on $115,200 at 5.50 percent
3. 15-year fixed on $400,000 at 6.25 percent with a second mortgage
4. 30-year adjustable on $73,432 at 7 percent
5. 15-year fixed on $328,000 at 5.75 percent

If the lender warrants that these five loans meet Fannie guidelines, then the new lender can buy those loans without having to individually approve the loans to make sure they meet lending guidelines.

LENDING GUIDELINES DEMYSTIFIED

Lending guidelines established by the secondary markets are many but the standard guidelines are as follows:

- ➤ Maximum loan amount acceptable
- ➤ Debt-to-income ratios
- ➤ Sufficient funds to close the transaction
- ➤ Minimum employment for two years
- ➤ Minimum credit standards

The buying and selling of mortgages has been streamlined to the point where mortgages are now a *commodity*. Even though one mortgage will seldom be exactly like the next one in terms of loan amount, credit, income, and so on, they are all alike because they fit the guidelines established by the secondary markets. Now these loans can be bought individually, called "flow" selling, or in big chunks where loans are packaged together, called "bulk" sales.

The secondary markets couldn't function as they do if each and every loan had to be scrutinized; there simply wouldn't be enough time to make the effort worthwhile. That would mean a lender would have to be very, very certain it not only wants to make that loan but also ties up its money for long periods of time.

If a mortgage loan is not a commodity that can be bought and sold quickly, there would be higher rates across the board for everyone. If, indeed, a product is a commodity, then lenders can compete against one another on the exact same product. Lenders would offer both a competitive rate and lower closing costs if they had to fight over the very same loan—much like any other business that bought and sold goods or services. If loans were all different, it would be impossible to evaluate them all.

Further, if loans couldn't be easily sold in the secondary markets, rates would be higher across the board, because a lender would be committed to tying up its money over the long haul—money it could invest in other categories when markets change. If, for example, a mortgage is made at 6 percent on a 30-year loan, that would tie up that money for 30 years or until the note was retired (if the owner sells the home or pays off the mortgage sooner).

Suppose the lender makes the decision and issues money at 6 percent for 30 years, but six months later the economy changes and lenders are issuing mortgage rates at 8 percent! Because the lender can't sell the mortgage, the lender is losing money every day—it could be making 2 percent more on its loans but can't because it is tied up in a 6 percent loan.

To offset such a scenario, a lender would price its mortgages artificially higher at the beginning to offset any potential increase in mortgages down the road. Or worse, not issue any fixed-rate mortgages whatsoever and only issue adjustable-rate mortgages. Adjustable-rate mortgages, or ARMs, can move up as interest rate markets move up. The predictability of a fixed-rate loan would no longer exist. Lenders would be forced to either price their mortgage higher or not issue fixed rates at all. We'll discuss how to pick the best mortgage loan in Chapter 6.

UNDERSTANDING CONVENTIONAL AND GOVERNMENT LOANS

Loans underwritten to Fannie and Freddie guidelines are called "conventional" loans, and loans underwritten to Ginnie Mae standards—VA, FHA, and USDA loans—are called "government" loans. Conventional loans can be "conforming" or "nonconforming." Conforming loans mean the loan itself does not exceed a specific amount, while nonconforming loans, called "jumbo" loans, are loans that are above conforming loan limits. Government loans can also have two categories of loans.

The difference between the two mortgage types, conventional and government, lies in who actually guarantees or warrants the mortgage loan. Individual lenders warrant conventional loans, while the federal government guarantees government loans. If a conventional loan goes into default, meaning the loan went bad and is either in foreclosure or otherwise foreclosed on, it's the individual lender who takes the hit. That means the lender has to write off or write down the value of that asset.

With a government loan, the government guarantees the performance of the note. As long as a lender issues the government loan in accordance with VA, FHA, or USDA guidelines, the government compensates the lender by buying that loan, taking it off the lender's books.

What if a lender buys a conventional loan and it goes into default? As long as the loan was underwritten per conventional guidelines, then the buying lender can do nothing. But, if the loan was found to not have been underwritten in accordance with conventional guidelines, the original lender will "*repurchase*" the bad loan due to a buying/selling contract between the two lenders. For instance, a loan might have been approved that required the buyer to have been self-employed for at least two years but the lender made a mistake and approved the loan without verification of two years of self-employment, typically evidenced by two years filed tax returns. Or a loan could require that the buyer put down 5 percent of his own funds in the transaction, but it was later discovered that the buyer borrowed the money from a friend and pretended the money was his.

In either instance, due to an underwriting mistake by the lender or fraud by the borrower, the unfortunate lender would be forced to buy that loan back with funds it no longer had because it used the funds from selling the first mortgage to issue another.

If a few of these scenarios occur, the lender is no longer in business.

When a government loan is foreclosed on, the government guarantees that note and typically sells the property at an auction or through prearranged sales. If you've ever heard of the term "HUD foreclosure sale" then you've just heard how the government can get its money back when it is forced to reimburse a lender for a loan that went bad. Of course, if there was fraud involved or the lender made an underwriting mistake, then the lender might still be forced to buy back the offending loan.

As discussed in Chapter 1, mortgage loan guidelines have changed over the years and now look totally different than they did just a short time ago. What has changed, and how do you qualify with these new changes?

CHANGES TO THE MAXIMUM LOAN AMOUNT

The current maximum conforming loan amount is at $417,000. In fact, it's been at that level for more than three years. What makes this unique is how loan limits are established and what constitutes a conforming and a jumbo loan.

Historically, in each October of every year, the Office of Housing and Economic Development would calculate the current, average home price in the United States and compare it to the previous year. If the home price increased by 8 percent over the previous year, then the maximum conforming loan amount would be increased by 8 percent.

This happened year after year, every year. Interestingly enough, home prices typically showed some type of increase the previous year. Therefore, the loan limits were increased. Then in the late 2000s, home prices started to decline. This happened as the housing bubble was just about to burst. The loan limits looked as if they'd actually be lowered instead of being increased or held steady. If loan limits dropped, that would put more people out of buying a home, slowing an already-damaged housing market. Instead of decreasing the loan limits, the government left maximum conforming limits the same, where they are today.

SUPER-CONFORMING LOANS

The next question is how high jumbo mortgages can go that can still be considered conventional, or loans that can be bought or sold by banks or Fannie and Freddie.

This is also a major change. Historically, jumbo mortgages meant anything above the current conforming limit. Now, however, jumbo carries a new moniker- "super-conforming."

Super-conforming means the loan amount is above the conforming limit yet still available for purchase and sale in the secondary market. In the past, private agencies were established that bought and sold jumbo loans in the secondary market, but these went away in 2007.

These private agencies performed the same functions as Fannie and Freddie did, and with them came some very affordable interest rates—typically, only about 0.25 percent higher than a conforming loan. If a rate for a $300,000 loan could be had on the open market for 6.00 percent, then a loan in the amount of $500,000 could be found for, say, 6.25 percent. But that tiny spread soon died with the demise of the private secondary market for jumbo mortgages.

This created a void in the jumbo market, temporarily halting jumbo activity. Soon thereafter, Fannie and Freddie both entered the jumbo market by buying loans above the $417,000 conforming limit.

Because of their entry in the jumbo market, the buying and selling of jumbo loans could occur again, with the new limits set at $625,500 if you lived in a high-cost area. *High cost* is determined by multiplying the median sales price of homes in your area by 1.25. If that number exceeds $417,000 then you qualify for the conventional jumbo loan up to $625,500.

But now the differences between a conforming rate and a jumbo rate are closer to a full percentage point instead of a quarter percent. If you can find a conforming rate at 6.00 percent then that same lender could offer a jumbo loan at 7.00 percent.

That means if you bought a home for $500,000 and had only 10 percent down, your loan amount would be $450,000, requiring an increase in interest rate by a full percentage point, even though the conforming loan amount was just about $30,000 less than the amount you're borrowing.

There are ways to overcome this issue, as we'll discuss in detail in Chapter 6, but as you can see, these changes have affected homes in higher priced areas much more so than others.

CHANGES TO CREDIT SCORE UNDERWRITING

You've heard about them. In fact if you turn on the television, the radio, or peruse the Internet you're likely to witness at least one advertisement talking about credit and credit scores.

Exactly what are credit scores? Scores are a numerical value placed on the likelihood of someone defaulting on a loan. The lower the score, the greater the likelihood of default. Default can mean making a payment more than 30 days past the due date of the bill or not paying at all.

Credit scoring really hit the mortgage scene in the late 1990s, when they were used as an additional risk-evaluation tool. In fact, up until 2008, minimum credit scores weren't required for most conventional and government loans. As long as a loan was approved with an automated underwriting system, or AUS, the credit score mattered little. Nothing, in some instance. We'll examine the AUS in more detail in Chapter 4.

But how are credit scores calculated? Do employees at the credit bureau look at your credit report and assign a number? Not exactly, but your credit score will reflect previous payment patterns.

The credit score used by mortgage lenders was developed by a company called Fair Isaac Corporation, or FICO. All three credit bureaus (Experian, Equifax, and TransUnion) use the FICO scoring model. Your credit history assigns a certain number of "points" that make up your credit score. Or more correctly, it deducts points from your total number of available points for cracks in your credit. Credit scores can range from a low of 350 (I've never seen one that low) to 850 (I've never seen one that high, either). Perfect credit is 850. As different business and other companies that have issued credit to you report your payment patterns, your credit score will emerge.

So if there are three credit bureaus, Equifax, Experian, and TransUnion, are your credit scores all the same? That's highly unlikely, and here's why. These three bureaus are nothing more than repositories—they're holders of data. When a business opens up a credit account for a borrower, the business reports various things about the credit account to the bureau. How much you borrowed, how much your payments were, if you were ever late and by how much, and so on. In exchange for reporting this information to the credit bureau, the business can also pull credit histories on its potential customers to see how they paid in the past with other businesses.

IMPROVING YOUR CREDIT SCORE

Credit scores comprise five major components, each with its own weight.

35 percent of your score is made up of your payment patterns.
30 percent of your score is made up of your available credit.
15 percent of your score is made up of how long you've had credit.
10 percent of your score is made up of credit inquiries.
10 percent of your score is made up of the types of credit accounts.

You start with the potential of 850, and then the points start coming off. Here are some ways you can improve your credit score.

Improve Your Payment Patterns

This is the easiest to understand; it simply means paying on time. Technically, it means not being more than 30 days late. Being more than 30 days past your due date will immediately harm your score, and points will be deducted.

Being more than 60 days late hurts even more than a 30-day late payment. And 90 days? Worse still. When loans get past 90 days late, they can be "charged off" by the original creditor, deeming the account no longer collectable. That's how a credit bureau reports your payments, in terms of 30-day increments. By keeping a history of not having late payments over time, your credit scores will rise.

One important note: Credit accounts can have penalties when a payment is not made on or before the due date. Even if you haven't made a payment 30 days past the due date, while that information won't be reported negatively to the credit bureaus as a late payment, indeed the creditor will regard a payment made past the due date as a negative and charge you higher rates, fees, or both. So to the best of your ability, pay your bills on time. They will affect your mortgage.

Control Your Available Credit to the Secret Ratio

The second most important score component is that of available credit. Put another way, how much are your current loan balances compared to your credit lines available to you?

For instance, if you have a credit card with a limit of $10,000 and a $5,000 balance, your available credit is 50 percent. If you have a $3,000 balance, then your available credit is 70 percent of your limit. It then follows that a zero balance gives you a 100 percent available.

But within all these percentages lies a secret ratio, 33 percent. By keeping your current credit balances at or around approximately one-third of your available credit, your credit scores will improve. As your balances grow and approach your credit limits, your scores will begin to deteriorate.

Let's say your current balance is $3,000 and your credit card limit is at $10,000. Your credit scores will constantly rise over time. The longer you keep your balances at or around one-third of your limits, the better your scores will be.

Then you decide to take a vacation, but instead of paying cash for it or putting it on your debit card, you elect to pay for it on your credit card that has the $10,000 credit limit. The vacation costs $5,000 and you put that $5,000 on your card. Add that $5,000 to the $3,000 balance you already had, and your new balance is $8,000, or 80 percent of your available credit. If you paid off that balance before you got your next statement, your scores might not take a hit, but if your new 80 percent balance is reported to the three credit bureaus, then your credit scores will drop. Worse still, should you not only approach 100 percent of your available credit but also go over your limits, your scores will be harmed further still.

What happens to your scores if you pay your balances off completely instead of keeping a balance? Oddly, your scores will drop instead of rise. It sounds odd at first glance, but if you think about it for a moment, it does make sense.

Remember that scores are an indicator of a possible loan default, and how would a lender know if you were likely to repay a debt if there were no debt to pay off? In other words, can you not only be approved for credit but be able to pay that debt back when due? Would you make your payments before the due date? After the due date? Would you pay the minimum, or would you pay the balances off entirely?

If you never charged anything or never used credit, then you haven't shown, at least to the credit bureaus, that you can responsibly handle credit accounts.

Think Before You Close an Account

Closing accounts can also harm your credit score. That's right, what might seem to be a responsible move at first glance can actually lower your score. Let's look at that magical percentage again of 33 percent.

If your credit limit is at $10,000 and you've had this account for a while, then your scores will begin to reflect that account history. If you've charged some things then responsibly paid them back over time, then your scores will improve. But if you paid off that balance and then canceled that account, suddenly you don't have the credit limit anymore.

Your available credit, which ideally should be around 33 percent, is now at 100 percent—exactly the same percentage as if you charged up your credit card to the $10,000 limit. Your credit limit is zero and your balance is zero.

Your scores will drop in this example. I know that old school thinking, and I think I would agree, is to close old accounts you no longer use. That makes sense to me for a variety of reasons, one of which is to limit the possibility of identity theft. But closing unused accounts will drop scores.

This quirk comes into play in a different way when we look at another example.

Let's say we have three credit cards with a $10,000 total credit line, with each card carrying a $3,333 limit. If the total balance is $3,000, then the balances are at 30 percent of your available credit. That's good.

Now close one of those accounts by transferring the balance to another card that might have a lower interest rate. So you transfer a balance and close out one of those cards and you still have a $3,000 balance, but by closing one account you've lowered your credit limit from $10,000 to $6,666.

By comparing your balance, which remained constant, with your new, lower credit limit, that percentage works to 45, which is a $3,333 balance and a $6,666 limit. Your scores will begin to drop as your balances approach half of your credit limit when all you did was take a prudent move and transfer a balance with a higher rate to another card and close the old account.

Now take that one step further and close one more account, leaving you with a $3,333 balance and a $3,000 limit. Your scores will take a huge negative hit because not only did your available credit disappear, but you also exceeded your limits.

There were recent changes in this formula that caused FICO to adjust its algorithms. It became evident that the more available credit one had when compared to the balances, as long as those balances were at 33 percent of available credit, the scores would increase. So someone found out that an "authorized user" of a credit card could take advantage of the credit history of the account they were authorized on.

An authorized user is someone who isn't ultimately responsible for paying the credit card debt but has the authority to charge things on the card. This is common, for instance, with a college student who has a credit card with her name on it but the account really belongs to her parents. The daughter who had no established credit or poor credit scores could increase her scores by "borrowing" her parents credit history by being added as an authorized user.

If you pay attention to your payment history and your available credit, you'll have mastered your credit scores.

Rely on Length of Credit History

The length of credit history represents 15 percent of your score. The longer you've had credit accounts that have reported to the credit bureaus, the better your credit score will be. Even if you've had some late payments in the past or had your available credit lines reduced, the longer-term impact of other negative credit items will be lessened.

Limit Credit Inquiries

A credit inquiry means some other company has looked at your credit report either with or without your express permission. A common example of a permitted credit inquiry, an inquiry with your permission, is when you might apply for an automobile loan. You shop for a car, then apply for a car loan. Or you do that in reverse—either way, you give a business your permission to review your credit history.

Each time a business reviews your credit in order to make a credit decision that you requested, it will lower your credit score. Multiple credit inquiries could be an indicator that someone is in or soon will be in financial straits.

There are some consumer protection features that help protect your credit score if you apply for credit in multiple places if your credit request is for the same transaction and within a relatively narrow period of time.

Say you're shopping for a new boat and you want to finance it. You go to the boat store and you apply for credit there. You call your credit union that same day and apply for credit there, as well. In this example, there would only be one credit inquiry and it would not be counted as multiple ones, which would drive down your score.

However, if you applied for a boat loan at the boat store, thought about it for a few weeks and then called your credit union again and applied for credit once more, then you can expect your scores to fall.

The same thing can happen when applying for a mortgage with multiple lenders. As long as your inquiries are within a relatively short time frame, typically within 30 days, then the scoring models will consider that as a single inquiry because it's for a single transaction. If you applied for a mortgage to buy a home, then six months later decided to refinance, that would be considered multiple transactions and again drop your scores. There are credit inquiries that don't affect your credit score at all; these are called "soft" inquiries.

The most common soft inquiry is when a consumer checks his own credit to review for any errors or to simply get an update on what his credit report looks like. When a consumer checks his own credit it's not considered a "hard" inquiry that would indicate someone was applying for more credit.

Another example of a soft inquiry is when an employer might check someone's credit as part of its hiring process. Or a credit card company that is expanding its customer base would access a consumer's credit report to decide whether to offer a new credit card. Both of these instances are considered soft and won't affect a credit score one way or another.

Pay attention to when you have credit inquiries made. If they are made close together and for the same purpose, you likely won't get hit.

Recognize That Different Types of Credit Can Hurt or Help

There are different types of credit issued, based on what is being collateralized (if anything) and the type of company issuing the credit. A bank issuing a mortgage is considered the top-tier credit account both because it's for a mortgage and not a boat, for instance, and also because it's made from a retail lending institution that offers credit cards, checking accounts, and savings accounts primarily to those with good credit.

Another top-tier credit account would be an automobile loan or some other tangible or secured asset.

Credit cards can positively impact a credit account as long as they're also issued by lenders who primarily make loans to those with good credit. For those with not-so-good credit, there are finance companies that make loans to those with either less than perfect credit or no credit at all. Although a credit score can benefit with a positive payment history on a loan obtained through a finance company, it won't be impacted as much if the same credit line were issued by a bank or credit union.

Finally, there is one other type of credit: alternative credit.

Use Alternative Credit

Alternative credit accounts have changed over the years and can now be part of a credit report just as any other trade line. Alternative credit is made up of things such as paying rent on time, or paying a cell phone or cable TV bill on time, each and every month.

Cable TV companies and cell phone companies, just like other utility accounts such as electricity, water, and telephone, don't report consumers' payment history to the credit bureaus. There are no 30-, 60-, or 90-day late payments that would show up on your credit report in the same way as an automobile loan would. Their emergence as a legitimate credit source, however, has helped consumers become homeowners who hadn't established a traditional credit history with credit cards or automobile loans.

So who would use alternative credit? There are two types: those who haven't yet established credit in the traditional fashion and those who refuse to use credit cards and only use their debit cards or cash/emergency funds.

NEW UNDERWRITING REQUIREMENTS REGARDING CREDIT

It is important for you to be able to provide appropriate credit history because recent changes in Fannie and Freddie guidelines now make it a requirement that at least three trade lines plus rent be reflected on a credit report with activity in the last 12 months.

In the past, consumers would only need to provide 12 months of canceled checks along with their pay history from say, their cable bill, and then a person at the mortgage company would verify the information and include that documentation in the loan application package. There was no need to report it to the credit bureau. And even if there were, it was a tedious process for the credit bureau to enter the information manually onto the credit report. This is no longer true.

GETTING ALTERNATIVE CREDIT ON YOUR CREDIT REPORT

The process of getting alternative credit on your credit report is relatively easy, although not as easy as simply pulling a credit report. Instead, the consumer gives the lender the contact information for a landlord, the electricity, phone, and water companies, or other monthly obligations that are provided by third parties. Cell phone bills, Internet access, insurance payments—it could include anything that is paid to a third party on a monthly basis that can be independently verified.

The lender contacts the phone company and asks for a 12-month payment history. The phone company provides that payment history and shows how many, if any, monthly payments have been more than 30 days past their due date.

The lender collects the three accounts plus the landlord information and forwards it to the credit bureaus, which enter the information on the credit report. Now the credit report accurately reflects the alternative credit while at the same time complying with lender requirements of having a credit report containing three trade lines plus rent over the previous 12 months.

ESTABLISHING APPROPRIATE ACCOUNTS (AND A SECRET ALTERNATIVE IF YOU DON'T)

What if a borrower doesn't have three accounts in addition to rent? What if the borrower only has two accounts, such as rent and a cell phone? This is common for someone who lives in an apartment building with most or all of the utilities included in the rent.

In this example, there really is no way around the minimum accounts required by mortgage companies. The borrower must establish new accounts for a 12-month period. This can also affect those who live with their parents or otherwise rent-free.

There is one other type of account that can work, but you'll need to check with your potential lender ahead of time, because not all lenders accept this account: regular savings. A regular savings account, or other type of investment account, can work as an alternate credit type under certain conditions:

➤ The payments must be made at least once every 90 days.

➤ The account may not have any withdrawals over the previous 12 months.

➤ The amounts must be regular, significant amounts.

➤ The account must be voluntary and not forced.

Most such accounts are savings plans that take out a certain amount of money each month from a checking account and transfer it to a savings account. The account must also grow and not be depleted. Depositing money and then withdrawing it doesn't show any diligent pay history to that account.

The payments must be regular in nature—meaning once per month, every month, or once per quarter—and also be "significant" in nature, meaning that someone who makes $5,000 per month won't get too much credit for a $5 per month savings plan.

Finally, the payment must be voluntary and not forced. An example of a forced payment is a regular monthly contribution to a 401(k) plan, where the funds are deposited directly into a 401(k) account instead of given to the consumer who then deposits those funds into a savings account.

Someone with an active 401(k) account can't suddenly start and stop their contributions at will; it's not voluntary in that manner. Employees can certainly change their contributions when they're told they are able to by their employer, but this isn't considered voluntary.

But if you don't have an active, voluntary, regular savings account with no withdrawals for the past 12 months, you'll need to start one if you need an additional alternative account.

CHANGES TO UNDERWRITING IN REGARD TO CREDIT SCORES

If you're about to apply for a credit card, the credit company won't make a bunch of phone calls to people and businesses that you have credit with but will instead contact one or more of the credit bureaus to see how you paid those accounts in the past. This is done electronically by providing the business with a number, your credit score.

These three bureaus are located in different parts of the country. Some businesses subscribe to all three bureaus and some to just one. It costs a business money to subscribe to each individual bureau, and sometimes these businesses don't feel the need to check with all three bureaus that are geographically scattered across the United States but, rather, trust that if you've got good credit at one bureau, then the likelihood of you having good credit at the other bureaus is high.

If a business only uses one bureau, then that bureau will be the only repository to receive credit histories from that business. A business may use Experian but not TransUnion, for example, on a regular basis. As credit histories mature and credit scores begin to form, the different bureaus will most likely have different scores—similar scores, but different nonetheless. Mortgage companies use all three credit bureaus when making a mortgage decision, and the scores might look something like this:

Experian	726
Equifax	699
TransUnion	719

Even though all three use the same FICO scoring engine to create these scores, because they all contain slightly different credit information, the credit number will be different.

A lender will throw out the highest number and the lowest number and use the middle one. In this example, the score from TransUnion at 719 will be the score used for the mortgage credit decision.

Now let's look at a couple borrowing together.

Credit Bureau	Borrower A	Borrower B
Experian	726	675
Equifax	699	618
TransUnion	719	602

If there are two people on the same loan, which credit score does the lender use? It used to be that the lender would use the middle credit score of the "breadwinner" or the person who made the most money in the household. This is no longer true. Now a lender uses the borrower with the lowest aggregate credit scores and uses the middle score. Sometimes this can cause a loan to be denied due to damaged credit or could perhaps penalize the applicants with a higher rate, fees, or both. We'll examine how to overcome this particular obstacle in Chapter 8.

REPAIRING YOUR CREDIT SCORE

Although credit scores have always been important, they have never become more so since lending guidelines changed in 2008. Now credit scores can directly impact your mortgage rate.

In the past, there was no such thing as a minimum credit score as long as one got an approval using an automated underwriting system. Not only that, but someone with a lower score could get the very same interest rate as someone with a near-perfect credit score. For instance, an automated underwriting approval would take into consideration a variety of factors such as debt-to-income ratios, equity in the property, assets, and any number of things that would come to make a financial portfolio of a mortgage applicant.

How can a borrower with a 580 credit score get the very same interest rate as someone with an 800 score? It does seem a bit illogical to have credit scores in the first place if it has no impact on the mortgage rate.

If, however, there were other compensating factors that played into the approval equation, that could mean someone with a 580 score could get a 6.00 percent rate, the very same rate an 800 score borrower could get. If the 580 borrower had tons of equity in his house, it would offset the lower credit score. For example, if the house appraised at $500,000 and the loan amount was only $100,000, a borrower would be less likely to default on a mortgage by giving up all that equity through foreclosure. This is the reasoning, anyway.

If, by contrast, that same borrower with a 580 credit score tried to borrow $450,000 on a $500,000 home, then the loan would typically be declined with an automated underwriting system.

THE NEW MODEL FOR QUALIFYING: THE LOAN LEVEL PRICING ADJUSTMENT (LLPA)

For nearly a decade, credit scores had little impact on a loan approval other than being an indicator of the likelihood of default. But that changed. Now lenders use a model designed by Fannie and Freddie called the *loan level pricing adjustment*, or *LLPA*. Bye-bye, zero-down mortgage!

Established in December 2008, the LLPA is a complicated yet strict guideline that, for the first time, combines a credit score with an equity position to determine not simply a loan approval (the automated underwriting system does that), but to determine the interest rate issued for that loan as well.

The LLPA is fluid and can change based on how current credit markets are behaving. In good economic times, the LLPA grid can be relaxed, and in more difficult economic times, the grid will be more restrictive. The chart on the facing page is a typical LLPA grid.

Confusing? Of course it is, at first glance. This is the chart lenders use to adjust your interest rate, depending on a combination of credit scores and your down payment, or equity, position. There are

Conventional Fixed Price Adjustments (Does not apply to terms 15 yrs or less or My Community)

Credit Score	<=60%	>60-<=70%	>70-<=75%	>75-<=80%	>80-<=85%	>85-<=90%	>90-<=95%	>95-<=97%
>=740	(0.250)	0.000	0.000	0.000	0000	0.000	0.000	0.000
720-739	(0.250)	0.000	0.000	0.250	0.000	0.000	0.000	0.000
700-719	(0.250)	0.500	0.500	0.750	0.500	0.500	0.500	0.500
680-699	0.000	0.500	1.000	1.500	1.000	0.750	0.750	0.750
660-679	0.000	1.000	2.000	2.500	2.250	1.750	1.750	n/a
640-659	0.500	1.250	2.500	3.000	2.750	2.250	2.250	n/a
620-639	0.500	1.500	3.000	3.000	3.000	2.750	2.750	n/a
< 620	0.500	1.500	3.000	3.000	3.000	3.000	3.000	n/a

Cash Out Refinance Adjustments (in addition to adjustments above; does apply to 15 yr terms)

Credit Score	<=60%	>60-<=70%	>70-<=75%	>75-<=80%	>80-<=85%	>85-<=90%	>90-<=95%	>95-<=97%
>=740	0.000	0.250	0.250	0.500	0.625	n/a	n/a	n/a
720-739	0.000	0.625	0.625	0.750	1.500	n/a	n/a	n/a
700-719	0.000	0.625	0.625	0.750	1.500	n/a	n/a	n/a
680-699	0.000	0.750	0.750	1.375	2.500	n/a	n/a	n/a
660-679	0.250	0.750	0.750	1.500	n/a	n/a	n/a	n/a
640-659	0.250	1.250	1.250	2.250	n/a	n/a	n/a	n/a
620-639	0.250	1.250	1.250	2.750	n/a	n/a	n/a	n/a
<620	1.250	2.250	2.250	2.750	n/a	n/a	n/a	n/a

two charts here, one for a standard mortgage and one for a mortgage refinance loan that pulls equity out of the property.

To use the chart, first find your credit score. Then find where it would fit in the very first column on the left-hand side titled "Credit Score." Next review the following columns that are headed < = 60%, >60% < 70%, . . . and so on. These columns express your loan amount compared to the value of the property, or LTV, which means *loan to value*.

On the very far right, you'll see >95%< = 97%. This means the loan amount is at or above 95 percent of the value of the home but less than or equal to 97 percent of the value of the home.

If the value of the home is $100,000 and your loan amount was $96,000, then this would be your column. Next, find your credit score and match it up on the far-left-hand column. Find your score, then move over to the right for the appropriate LTV.

If your credit score is 681, your loan amount is $96,000 and your value is $100,000 then your rate adjustment is 0.75 points. Stay with me here.

Let's say you have a credit score of 724 and you have 25 percent down. Then find your appropriate credit score row then move over to the column labeled >70%< =75%. You'll notice the adjustment is 0.00, or zero adjustment to the rate.

The impact of the LLPA is this: If you have no rate adjustments according to the LLPA and the going market rate for a 30-year mortgage is 6.00 percent at zero points, then that's your rate, according to the LLPA matrix.

If, however, your loan amount is at 96 LTV and your credit score is 681, then your rate would be 6.00 percent with an additional 0.75 points. One point equals 1 percent of your loan amount, so in this example your additional fees in the form of points is 0.75 percent of $96,000, or $720.

Now let's take it one step further and say your loan amount is $96,000 but your credit score is 679. When you find your credit score in the appropriate row, then follow all the way across to the >95%<=97% column. You'll see no adjustments at all. Nothing but a line where the adjustment is supposed to be.

 If there is a line and no adjustment, that means you can't get approved with your current credit score and down payment.

IMPORTANCE OF CREDIT SCORES

This is the first time that credit scores have been used to decline a loan application. But not to fret, it may not be the end of the road. With your credit score of 679, you'll notice that if you travel one column to the left, you'll see an adjustment of 1.75, or 1.75 points. And by moving over one column, you'll also see that your LTV limits have fallen to > 90% < = 95%.

Now you can get your approval but you had to bring your loan amount equal to or below 95 percent of the property value and pay 1.75 points. On $95,000 you would get a 6.00 percent rate and pay 1.75 points, or $1,662.50.

We'll examine how rates are set and closing fees in detail in Chapter 8, but as you can see, the more risk the lender takes on in terms of credit and equity, the more the borrower will have to pay. This is for owner-occupied properties only.

CRITERIA FOR INVESTMENT PROPERTIES

Investment, or rental, properties are considered higher risk than a property that is occupied by the borrower. The reason is obvious in that, should a borrower who owns more than one property—his primary residence and some rental houses—ever fall into financial straits and has problems paying his mortgages then it's the primary residence that will be paid first. An investor will let rental properties be foreclosed on before he'll allow his primary residence to go.

Investment properties will also be priced with the LLPA but also add another fee, that for the property being an investment property versus a primary residence. Investment properties also require more down, as there is no such thing as a 3 percent down investment property mortgage. Conventional investor loans require a minimum of 20 percent down. In a purchase transaction with 20 percent down, the lender will add 2.25 points, or $2,250 on a $100,000 loan.

To see how the LLPA affects investment loans, first use the LLPA grid and take the credit score then find the appropriate LTV column. If the credit score is 655 with 20 percent down the adjustment would be 3.00 points for the score/LTV adjustment then add another 2.25 for putting down only 20 percent. That's a total of 5.25 points, or $5,250 in additional fees.

Using that very same scenario but with a 750 credit score, the adjustments would be 0.00 adjustment for credit score and 2.25 for 20 percent down. If the borrower puts 25 percent down instead of 20, the adjustments would again be 0.00 for the score and then 1.75 points for 25 percent down.

That's for a single-family residence. For a duplex or a two- to four-unit complex, there is an additional adjustment still. There is another 1.5 points added to the transaction.

This is the new world of mortgage pricing, and it can get confusing, even for the loan officer. If you've got a "technical" mortgage, which means that you've got an average credit score with minimal down and it's an investment property, make absolutely certain your loan officer is getting the numbers straight. You don't want to go down the merry little road and suddenly find out that you're required to pay an additional $2,000 the loan officer forgot to quote you. We'll discuss closing costs and disclosure requirements in detail in Chapter 8.

NEW RULES FOR REAL ESTATE INVESTORS

Fannie and Freddie both have new underwriting guidelines for investment properties, and it determines how many mortgages a person is allowed to have and still get a conventional loan.

In the past this has been a moving target, but both agencies have limited the number of financed properties a borrower might own. This has varied from as few as four properties to as many as ten, but the new guidelines spell out the requirements for both.

First, note that the guidelines are for financed properties—properties with loans against them. If the rule is that you can have only 10 financed properties, that doesn't mean you can't own 100 properties. You can. You just have to make sure that only 10 of them have loans on them and the others are free and clear.

The rules depend on how many financed properties you own. There are two new guidelines here that apply to someone with 1 to 4 financed properties then another set of rules for those with 5 to 10 financed properties.

Anyone can finance up to four properties with few restrictions, other than the requirement that the owner can qualify based on credit and income. A common question for the novice real estate investor is, "Can I use the rental income from the property I'm about to buy to help me qualify for a loan?" The answer depends on whether the borrower is an experienced real estate investor or has rental properties that he collects rent and pays mortgages on. In the case of a new investor who only owns his own home and the mortgage that goes along with it and then decides to buy a rental property, a lender will not allow the borrower to use the rental income to help him qualify. There is no history of being a landlord and managing the real estate asset.

Say the rental property yields $2,000 per month in rent and the new mortgage payment would only be $500. Then that would leave $1,500 per month in additional income. But if the borrower needs that additional $1,500 per month in income in order to qualify for the new loan, without having been a seasoned real estate investor, the lender won't allow that income to help qualify for the new loan.

By contrast, if someone has owned rental properties or currently owns them, then the lender would use that additional income to be realized from the new investment real estate in order to help qualify the borrower if that income is needed.

How would a lender know that one way or another? The lender will ask for tax returns and look for what is called the IRS Schedule E, which shows real estate transactions for that tax year. When someone owns rental properties, the rental income and expenses are reported on the Schedule E portion of their tax return. A lender won't simply take someone's word for it.

These changes have turned the conventional underwriting world upside down, as lenders tightened their lending guidelines and Fannie and Freddie both have been overhauled in every aspect of their mortgage lending, from the maximum loan amounts to minimum down payment requirements.

SUMMARY

> Fannie Mae and Freddie Mac provide liquidity in the mortgage marketplace. Lenders must conform to their guidelines if they want to continue making mortgage loans. These loans are called *conventional*.

> Guidelines place limits on maximum loan amounts, debt-to-income ratios, sufficient funds to close, and minimum employment and credit standards.

> Jumbo rates have risen dramatically compared to conventional conforming loans.

> For the first time, credit scores are required for a conventional mortgage.

> Credit scores are calculated using payment history, available

credit, length of credit history, credit inquiries, and types of credit used.

➢ There are legitimate tricks to improve your score.

➢ Alternative credit can be added to a credit report.

➢ Lenders pull credit scores from the three bureaus and use the middle score.

➢ LLPA is a significant change to the industry and combines credit scores with equity position to price a rate for a borrower.

➢ Limits are placed on real estate investors.

Government-Backed Loans: VA, FHA, and USDA

NOW THAT WE'VE COVERED the conventional lending guidelines, let's explore the new ways the federal, state, and local governments can help with home loans. Government loans are not made by the government. Rather, they are "guaranteed" by the government. Guaranteed, that is, unless the loan doesn't meet established lending guidelines. Lenders will approve a government loan individually and can turn around and sell that same loan on the secondary market just like a conventional loan and for the very same reasons.

Unlike conventional loans, government-backed loans are not used for investment purposes but for owner-occupied residences only. Government-backed loans are for your primary residence and can be a single-family residence (a house), a duplex, triplex, or four-plex, and a condominium or townhouse. Government-backed loans are typically targeted toward a specific class of borrower—be it a veteran or a first-time homebuyer or someone buying in a specific geographical area.

Government loans are guaranteed with a fee that the borrower pays in conjunction with each loan that is made. VA loans, for instance, have a "funding" fee of about 2.00 percent of the loan amount that is included on each and every VA loan. FHA loans have a mortgage insurance premium, or MIP, and USDA loans require a 2 percent guarantee fee. For instance, on a $200,000 VA loan, there would be a funding fee of around $4,000 that is part of the VA loan package. It's this funding fee that is used by the VA to reimburse a lender for part of its losses should the loan default. In reality, this funding fee is nothing more than an insurance policy, paid by the borrowers to benefit the lenders.

FHA loans have an MIP that is paid both upfront at the very beginning of the loan and also in a monthly premium paid each month. These funds, too, are used to offset losses incurred when loans go into default.

Government loans have been around for a long time, and their guidelines rarely change. That's one of the main reasons government-backed loans were spared most of the bloodshed during the mortgage market meltdown in 2007 and 2008. Lenders can add their own twists to government loans, but in general, one VA loan made at Lender A is identical in underwriting nature to a VA loan made at Lender B.

VA LOANS

The Department of Veterans Affairs controls various veterans' benefits, ranging from education to medical care to housing. It's here that the VA loan is guaranteed. VA loans are available to qualified veterans and eligible members of the National Guard. They allow the veteran to buy real estate with no money down at market rates.

Many Borrowers Are Eligible for VA Loans

Who is eligible for a VA loan? More than you would think. It's not only for those who have retired from the armed forces. Here are the eligibility criteria.

Service During Wartime

    WWII: September 16, 1940, to July 25, 1947

    Korean: June 27, 1950, to January 31, 1955

    Vietnam: August 5, 1964, to May 7, 1975

You must have at least 90 days on active duty and been discharged under other than dishonorable conditions. If you served less than 90 days, you may be eligible if discharged for a service-connected disability.

Service During Peacetime

    July 26, 1947, to June 26, 1950

    February 1, 1955, to August 4, 1964

    May 8, 1975, to September 7, 1980 (Enlisted)

    May 8, 1975, to October 16, 1981 (Officer)

You must have served at least 181 days of continuous active duty and been discharged under other than dishonorable conditions. If you served less than 181 days, you may be eligible if discharged for a service-connected disability.

Service After September 7, 1980 (Enlisted), or October 16, 1981 (Officer)

If you were separated from service that began after these dates, you must meet at least one of these criteria:

    ➤ Completed 24 months of continuous active duty or the full period (at least 181 days) for which you were ordered or called to active duty and been discharged under conditions other than dishonorable.

    ➤ Completed at least 181 days of active duty and been discharged under the specific authority of 10 USC 1173 (Hardship), or 10 USC

1171 (Early Out), or have been determined to have a compensable service-connected disability.

➤ Been discharged with less than 181 days of service for a service-connected disability. Individuals may also be eligible if they were released from active duty due to an involuntary reduction in force, certain medical conditions, or, in some instances, for the convenience of the government.

Service During Gulf War

If you served on active duty during the Gulf War from August 2, 1990, to a date not yet determined, you must meet at least one of these criteria:

➤ Completed 24 months of continuous active duty or the full period (at least 90 days) for which you were called or ordered to active duty, and been discharged under conditions other than dishonorable.

➤ Completed at least 90 days of active duty and been discharged under the specific authority of 10 USC 1173 (Hardship), or 10 USC 1173 (Early Out), or have been determined to have a compensable service-connected disability.

➤ Been discharged with less than 90 days of service for a service-connected disability. Individuals may also be eligible if they were released from active duty due to an involuntary reduction in force, certain medical conditions, or, in some instances, for the convenience of the government.

Active Duty Service Personnel

If you are now on regular duty (not active duty for training), you are eligible after having served 181 days (90 days during the Gulf War) unless discharged or separated from a previous qualifying period of active duty service. You must also have at minimum 180 days remaining of service or show proof of reenlistment.

Selected Reserves or National Guard

You are eligible for a VA loan if you are not otherwise eligible but you have completed a total of six years in the Selected Reserves or National Guard (member of an active unit, attended required weekend drills and two-week active duty for training) and meet one of these criteria:

- ➤ Were discharged with an honorable discharge
- ➤ Were placed on the retired list
- ➤ Were transferred to the Standby Reserve or an element of the Ready Reserve other than the Selected Reserve after service characterized as honorable service
- ➤ Continue to serve in the Selected Reserves

Individuals who completed less than six years may be eligible if discharged for a service-connected disability.

You may also be determined eligible if you meet one of these criteria:

- ➤ Are an unremarried spouse of a veteran who died while in service or from a service-connected disability
- ➤ Are a spouse of a serviceperson missing in action or a prisoner of war

Note: Also, a surviving spouse who remarries on or after attaining age 57, and on or after December 16, 2003, may be eligible for the home loan benefit. However, a surviving spouse who remarried before December 16, 2003, and on or after attaining age 57, must apply no later than December 15, 2004, to establish home loan eligibility. VA must deny applications from surviving spouses who remarried before December 6, 2003, that are received after December 15, 2004.

Eligibility may also be established for the following:

> Certain United States citizens who served in the armed forces of a government allied with the United States in WWII

> Individuals with service as members in certain organizations, such as Public Health Service officers, cadets at the United States Military, Air Force, or Coast Guard Academy, midshipmen at the United States Naval Academy, officers of National Oceanic and Atmospheric Administration, merchant seaman with WWII service, and others

You Still Have to Qualify to Get a VA Loan

The VA loan is without a doubt the best available resource for a home loan if the borrower is needing or wanting a low- to no-down-payment loan. Conventional loans, for instance, require a minimal down payment—as little as 3 percent—but even with such a small amount down, the mortgage insurance is sometimes prohibitive.

With a VA loan amount of $200,000 at 6 percent over 30 years, the principal and interest payment is $1,199 per month. A conventional loan with the minimum 3 percent down not only would have an increase in rate due to the LLPA, but also would require a mortgage insurance premium. With a credit score of 680, on a $200,000 loan, the rate would be adjusted to 6.375 percent.

The principal and interest payment would be $1,247 per month. Now add the PMI payment of $197, and the monthly payment is $1,444 per month. That's $245 more each month! If you can get the VA loan, it is definitely the way to go. But being eligible does not guarantee that you qualify.

VA home loans do not have a minimum credit score requirement. But VA lenders do, which is a new change to VA lending. In the past, as long as the loan was approved with an automated underwriting system, there was no credit score requirement. Now lenders require a minimum of 600 for a credit score, with some lenders requiring a 620 minimum score.

But what about the VA "guarantee?" Doesn't the qualifying veteran automatically get approved for a VA loan because of the guarantee? No.

One of the first things qualifying veterans must do when considering a VA home loan is to obtain their certificate of eligibility. This is a government-issued certificate that identifies the borrower as being eligible to receive a VA-guaranteed home loan.

The VA guarantee does not mean the veteran is preapproved for a VA loan. VA does require a good credit history among other underwriting requirements.

VA Loans Do Not Require a Credit Score—But VA Lenders Might!

Recall that in the last chapter, minimum credit scores for conventional loans were established for the first time in Fannie and Freddie history. Not so with VA loans, as the VA does not require a minimum score. However, the borrower must have established a good credit history, either with traditional credit or alternative credit. A "good" credit history simply means paying bills on time or at minimum not being more than 30 days late on any credit account.

It also means paying rent on time for a minimum of 12 months. It also means not going over your credit limit, not having any collection accounts or discharged credit accounts. One can have a bankruptcy in the past, but VA asks that the bankruptcy discharge be more than two years old with no more negative credit since the bankruptcy filing.

Typical credit patterns will be reflected in the credit score but since VA doesn't require a credit score, the credit report will be manually reviewed by a lender to make sure it complies with VA guidelines.

There is no rigid credit requirement. This means the loan may still be eligible if there is an outstanding collection account or there is a judgment that doesn't affect the property to be acquired. A judgment might mean there was a lawsuit and the borrower lost the law-suit and there is a monetary amount the borrower still owed. Although certainly a negative, it may not be imperative that the judgment or collection be paid off before a VA loan can be issued.

There is also no maximum number of late payments. There can be a 30-day late payment here and there. The VA doesn't require "no more than three 30-day late payments for rent and no more than two 30-day late payments for an automobile . . ." and so on.

But while the VA guidelines don't require a credit score minimum, that doesn't mean individual lenders won't now require a minimum score. Lenders can place minimum scores on VA loans as long as they don't discriminate in doing so. A lender can also have a credit score requirement in one state and not require a minimum score in another. A common lender minimum score can range from 580 to 620.

Automated vs. Manual Changes: Watch Those Ratios

Another VA guideline requires that the total housing payment, PITI, must be no more than 41 percent of the borrower's gross monthly income. This is a general guideline and not a hard and fast rule, but this is the number historically used to evaluate a VA home loan application.

For example, if a borrower's gross monthly income is $4,000, then 41 percent of that is $1,640, which is the maximum house payment. Anything higher than that and VA lenders get a little concerned when approving a loan. This 41 percent number is more strictly adhered to when the loan is underwritten manually instead of using an automated underwriting system, as explained in Chapter 4.

When a lender submits a VA loan for an approval, the lender will first use the automated underwriting system. Getting this approval can determine whether your loan is approved with a low credit score. For example, if you get an automated approval and your credit score is 560, since VA doesn't set a minimum score, some lenders will still accept that loan approval even though it's below their standard minimums. It's also now entirely possible to get an automated approval and still be rejected by the lender due to a credit score falling below the lender's minimums.

There's another new alternative when it comes to automated VA approvals, or at least what happens if the automated approval doesn't come through: the manual underwrite.

A *manual underwrite* means the loan is not approved with an automated underwriting system but everything is calculated manually. A manual underwrite will set strict limits on debt ratios, and lenders will use the VA ratio guideline of 41 percent as a rule and not a general guideline.

New VA Loan Limits Now Match Conventional Limits

Another welcome change in VA lending is how to calculate the veterans' home loan benefit. Historically, this benefit was calculated with an archaic system that was frankly hard to decipher. When veterans would receive their certificate of eligibility, this guarantee amount would be listed on the certificate, such as $12,500 maximum guarantee.

That would mean the VA would guarantee $12,500 of a VA loan, and four times that would be $50,000. The $50,000 would be the maximum VA loan. These guarantees would change over the years, gradually increasing with the value of current housing prices. Recent changes fixed all that.

The VA will guarantee 25 percent of a VA loan up to the conforming loan limits established by Freddie Mac. If the maximum conforming loan is $417,000, then the VA guarantee would be 25 percent of that, or $104,250.

Should the home loan default in any way, the VA would reimburse the lender for a maximum amount of $104,250, as long as the lender did everything properly when originally underwriting a VA loan.

This new method of establishing VA guarantees essentially placed a VA home loan on par with conventional mortgage loan limits and made them just as competitive—even more so when you consider it's a zero-down loan program.

The Secret VA Jumbo Loan Can Help Borrowers

Another twist in VA lending is the so-called "VA jumbo" mortgage loan. Recall that any loan amount above the conforming loan limit would be considered "jumbo" and subject to much higher rates. VA makes an exception, and it's a good one. Considering, of course, the borrower is VA qualified.

The current VA loan limit with zero down is $417,000, matching the conforming loan limits set by Fannie Mae and Freddie Mac. But the VA does make allowances for VA loans above that amount—way above. Say, around $700,000.

Current jumbo fixed rates are anywhere from 1.00 percent to 1.50 percent higher than conforming rates. That's a lot, and has many jumbo buyers in a quandary. A 30-year fixed conforming rate might be 6.00 percent, while a similar jumbo rate could be 7.50 percent. That spread used to not be so vast. Prior to the current mortgage mess, jumbo rates were typically about 0.25 to 0.50 percent higher than a conforming loan. But not so with a VA jumbo loan.

VA jumbo rates are near conforming rates, about 0.25 percent higher. And loans can be as high as $700,000. So how does this work?

VA Loans Are the Best No-Down Loans

First, if you're a qualified Veteran or Reservist, there simply is no better home loan out there with no money down. Period. Even when every lender on the planet was shouting "No Money Down!" for their home loans, it couldn't hold a candle to a VA loan when comparing rates and closing costs—as long as the VA loan didn't exceed $417,000 ($625,000 for Alaska and Hawaii).

Veterans Can Qualify for More Using a Quirk of the System

But a new little "quirk" in VA lending allows for VA loans above that $417,000 as long as the veteran comes up with some down payment—as with any jumbo mortgage.

To figure out how much down payment a veteran will need, simply multiply the amount of the sales price over $417,000 and take 25 percent of that. For instance, a home sells for $650,000. Now subtract the maximum "zero-down" VA loan amount of $417,000 and you get $233,000. Next, 25 percent of $233,000 is $58,250. That's the down payment needed from the veteran.

That works out to about 9 percent down payment on a $650,000 home. As on all VA loans, there is a funding fee of about 2.2 percent of the loan amount, but that can be rolled into the loan and not paid out of pocket. In this example, the final loan amount would be about $604,750. With a conventional jumbo loan, you would need 20 percent down and would pay a higher rate, say 7.50 percent compared to 6.25 percent.

Not all lenders will offer this program, so you'll need to do a little homework, and even those that do may have their own VA jumbo limits. But if you're in the jumbo market and are VA eligible, you should ask your lender if it participates in this unique program.

New Rules Remove Stigma of VA Loans

Another change in VA lending addresses closing costs. We'll discuss the types of closing costs and how to save on them in Chapter 8, but historically, the VA loan carried a bad rap because of the way it handled closing costs.

The VA home loan restricted the types of closing costs a borrower could incur. This policy was implemented to protect the veteran from unscrupulous lenders. This was certainly well intentioned, but it had a drawback: Who would wind up paying the closing costs on a loan that the veteran wasn't allowed to pay?

It could only come from two places: the seller or the lender.

The seller of a property who accepted an offer from someone using a VA loan would have to contend with paying additional closing fees from the sale proceeds. By itself, that wouldn't present a problem, but what if there were two offers on a home for the exact same price, one a VA and one a conventional offer?

The conventional offer would typically be the first one accepted because it was a better deal for the seller. If there were $1,000 worth of closing costs that the veteran wasn't allowed to pay for, then the seller would have to pay them. It's fairly simple really: The seller would take the offer that netted the most money and the veteran could lose out on a home he really wanted to buy.

Such closing costs are normally called "nonallowables" because the veteran isn't allowed to pay them. Veterans are allowed to pay for the appraisal, credit reports, title insurance and title-related services, origination fees or points, and for a survey. The acronym ACTOR was always a good way to remember which fees the veteran was allowed to pay out of pocket.

Anything else was off limits. Attorney fees, processing charges, underwriting fees, flood certificates, escrow charges—all of these fees could add up to an imposing amount.

The lender might also pay for the nonallowables by increasing the interest rate (as discussed in Chapter 8), but in reality when the lender does this the costs are simply transferred to the veteran in the form of a higher interest rate, resulting in higher payments.

But a new way of getting around this "nonallowable" requirement is for the veteran to pay a 1 percent origination fee, or 1 percent of the loan amount in lieu of the nonallowed fees. So instead of charging an attorney, processing, underwriting, and other nonallowable fees, the veteran simply pays a 1 percent origination fee at closing and the lender pays the nonallowable fees instead.

This might seem to be a bit of slight of hand that the VA would frown on, but in fact it's an approved method that the VA allows for. Why the VA wouldn't just cancel the nonallowable program altogether is beyond me, but that's how it works.

Is this unfair to the veteran, who now has to pay more in fees? I don't think so. Using the 1 percent origination fee method means the veteran pays no more and no less than someone using any other type of mortgage loan and still comes to the closing table with zero down payment. This new 1 percent method is seldom used because few VA loan officers know it's even available.

FHA LOANS

Along with VA loans, FHA loans are also guaranteed by a branch of the federal government. The Department of Housing and Urban Development, or HUD, oversees the Federal Housing Administration's mortgage loan program. Originally established in 1934 to help people buy homes and jump-start the economy, this program's popularity has waxed and waned over the years but now is the most popular of all government-backed mortgage programs.

The FHA guarantee program is financed with a mortgage insurance premium, or MIP. The MIP amount is set at 1.75 percent of the loan amount, so on a $200,000 loan, the MIP would be $3,500 and is a cost to the borrower.

There is also a monthly MIP amount paid by the borrower, typically 0.55 percent of the loan amount. It contributes to the FHA guarantee program. Again, on a $200,000 loan, 0.55 percent is $1,100, but this amount is paid monthly by the borrower, then forwarded to FHA on an annual basis. The monthly payment in this example is $1,100 divided by 12 months = $91.67 per month.

FHA does not have a zero-down program but it does have one that is close to it, requiring a minimum of 3.5 percent of the sales price as a down payment. And just like the VA loans, FHA does not approve the loan, an FHA lender does. As long as the loan was approved using proper FHA guidelines and the loan goes into default and the home is foreclosed on, the original lender will be compensated for its loss.

MIP Refunds Have Changed

Since 1983, MIP funds could be refunded to the borrower if the borrower retired the note before seven years had passed. If the borrower got an FHA loan and rolled in a $3,000 MIP and then sold that home the next year, retiring the note, the borrower would get a huge portion of that MIP back. Then in 2001, FHA changed the MIP refund rule to limit the refund to five years from seven.

The new change eliminates the refund altogether, regardless of the age of the loan, except when the mortgage loan is an FHA to FHA refinance, where the MIP refund is actually credited against the new MIP.

UPFRONT MORTGAGE INSURANCE PREMIUM REFUND PERCENTAGES

Year	Month of Year											
	1	2	3	4	5	6	7	8	9	10	11	12
1	80	78	76	74	72	70	68	66	64	62	60	58
2	56	54	52	50	48	46	44	42	40	38	36	34
3	32	30	28	26	24	22	20	18	16	14	12	10

This table shows that if the original FHA loan is two years and six months old when the loan is refinanced, then 46 percent of the original MIP amount will be refunded at the closing table as a credit to the brand new MIP required for the new FHA loan.

It used to be that the MIP refund would be applied as a credit or otherwise refunded for any loan that was replacing an FHA loan in a refinance, but no longer. FHA also had a refund program that gave back part of the original MIP if the loan was retired in any sense, either with a refinance or sale of the home. If a home with an FHA mortgage was sold, there could be some money back, but that went away with the new FHA guidelines.

Nehemiah Is Out of the Government Loan Business

If you're wondering who Nehemiah is, you would have to check out the Old Testament book by the same name. In the book of Nehemiah, the community of Israel came together to rebuild the walls of Jerusalem, and accomplished this enormous feat in 52 days. The Nehemiah Corporation of America was founded in 1994 based on an idea of assisting buyers who had trouble coming up with a down payment. Basically, HUD has severed its connection with the Nehemiah Program.

Nehemiah Corporation wasn't the only company that promoted this type of program, there were others. However, the Nehemiah was the first and the biggest. It was called a "seller assisted down payment" program because the seller would deposit a fee with Nehemiah who would then forward that fee to the settlement agent at closing. The loophole was that an FHA borrower could only get help for the down payment through a family member or a nonprofit organization, and Nehemiah was established as a nonprofit. In essence, it was money laundering to comply with FHA rules.

Problems began during the mortgage mayhem when it was discovered that seller-assisted down-payment loans had a higher default rate than for those who saved up their own down payment money.

When these programs were eliminated from FHA eligibility, it kept a lot of people out of buying a home when they couldn't come up with the funds.

FHA Loans Have Limits

Many consumers wrongly think that FHA is only for first-time buyers, but FHA loans are open to anyone who can qualify based on credit and income, as long as the loan amount is at or below established FHA limits.

FHA loan limits also have their own unique way of establishing maximum loan amounts, and unlike VA loans, those limits can vary from county to county. One can live in Austin, Texas, and have an FHA limit of $270,100, while 45 minutes away in San Antonio, Texas, the loan limits are $338,750.

FHA limits are established partially with consideration to the median sales price of the area, so the lower the value of homes that have sold in the previous year, the lower the maximum loan amount.

FHA loan limits, which can change annually, can be located directly on HUD's website at www.hud.gov. Simply type in your state and your county or parish and the maximum loan limits will appear for single family homes, duplexes, and two- to four-unit structures.

FHA also has its very own set of debt ratio requirements, but unlike the VA ratio, which is just one number, FHA has two: the housing ratio and the total debt ratio. The housing ratio is made up of principal, interest, taxes, insurance, and mortgage insurance. By dividing this number by the gross monthly income, you will arrive at the housing ratio. FHA likes to see this ratio be right at 29 percent.

If someone makes $5,000 per month in gross income, then the FHA rule asks that no more than 29 percent of $5,000 be dedicated to housing payments. In this case, the housing payment would be 29 percent of $5,000, or $1,450.

This is also how loan officers can determine how much a borrower can qualify for per FHA lending guidelines by taking the maximum housing amount and subtracting taxes, insurance, and mortgage insurance. The remaining figure is what can be dedicated to principal and interest. For example, let's say that of that $1,450, the property taxes are $200 per month, and both hazard and MIP payments are $50 each. That's $300 allotted to taxes and insurance payments, which leaves $1,150 available for principal and interest payment.

A loan officer then takes this figure and considers the length of the loan and current interest rates and finds out the resulting loan amount. Say that the loan is amortized over 30 years and current interest rates are at 6.00 percent.

By using the term, the rate, and the payment, the loan officer can arrive at the loan amount that works so the principal and interest payment would be about $191,810. That's how much FHA guidelines say this particular borrower could borrow.

But wait, FHA also has a total debt ratio to account for. This number is 41 percent. Total debt ratio takes the housing totals and adds consumer debt such as credit cards, automobile loans, student loans, and anything else that would appear on a credit report.

Still using this example, say the borrower has two car payments, each at $400 per month. By adding the two car payments totaling $800 to the current housing payment of $1,450, the total debt is $2,250.

If you divide $2,250 by $5,000 the answer is 45 percent. Slightly higher than FHA recommends. Not a deal killer, but a higher than normal debt ratio needs to be "offset" with other compensating factors such as good credit, assets in the bank, or job stability.

If the total debt ratio approached or exceeded 50, it's likely the loan would not get FHA approval with an automated underwriting system. If this were the case the file couldn't be approved with the automated underwriting system and the file will be underwritten manually (by a person) with very strict ratio limits of 45. So 41 is the guideline, 45 is the limit. We'll discuss the new dynamics of automated underwriting systems versus manual underwriting in Chapter 4.

FHA Changes Closing Costs

Recent changes in FHA guidelines have also been made regarding closing costs. FHA also had some built-in consumer protection laws that prohibited certain types of closing costs from being paid by the buyer. The FHA nonallowables were soon a thing of the past and there currently is no such thing as a nonallowable closing cost.

And unlike VA loans, these costs don't have to be made up with a 1 percent origination fee but only have to be similar and customary to closing costs for other conventional loans made in the area.

FHA Loans Now Have Minimum Credit Score Requirements

Like VA, FHA doesn't establish minimum credit scores for loans. Unlike VA, lenders don't pick and choose where they want to implement minimum credit score requirements. Lenders now require all loans have a minimum credit score of 620 whether the loan was underwritten manually or if approved with an automated underwriting system.

There Are Still Reverse Mortgages Available, but Only from FHA

FHA calls its reverse mortgage the Home Equity Conversion Mortgage, or HECM. Everyone else calls it a reverse mortgage. The biggest change in reverse mortgages is that the only current choice is the one from FHA. Fannie had its version of the reverse mortgage called the Homekeeper, but Fannie's program offered less to the client. Since FHA not only increased its reverse mortgage limits as well as lowering its costs, Fannie shut down its reverse program after being in existence for nearly two decades.

What Is a Reverse Mortgage?

Perhaps the easiest way to understand how a reverse mortgage works is to use some of the terminology that reverse mortgage loan officers use. Reverse lenders describe a mortgage as being either a "forward" or "reverse" home loan. A forward mortgage, which is any conventional or government home loan, is a mortgage taken out by the borrower, paid back monthly until the loan is ultimately paid off and the home is free and clear.

A reverse mortgage is issued by a mortgage company and is a lump sum, a monthly payment, a line of credit, or a combination of those so that it is giving the equity in the home to the homeowners immediately and is only paid off when the home is sold or the borrower moves out or passes away.

For instance, say a home is valued at $500,000 and the home is owned free and clear. A reverse mortgage would pay the homeowner a specified amount directly to the buyer that didn't have to be paid back every month.

This is compared to a "forward" mortgage, where the homeowner taps into the equity in the home with a home equity loan or a cash-out loan that refinances a current home loan and also pulls equity out of the home in the form of cash.

A forward mortgage has monthly payments that have to be paid back in regular installments. A reverse mortgage pulls equity out of the home, gives it to the homeowner, and doesn't have to be paid back every month—and not at all until the borrower no longer occupies the property.

Reverse mortgages are easy to qualify for. In fact, there is no minimum credit score, credit history, or even bankruptcies that affect the chances of getting a reverse mortgage. There are no debt ratios to contend with either.

A reverse mortgage can be a bit counterintuitive, but there really is no qualifying, other than age and equity limits. Since the borrower doesn't have to make monthly payments, there is no reason to calculate debt ratios. The loan is paid back when the borrower no longer occupies the property.

And since payment histories are not a consideration, then credit is not an issue either. Instead, the funds are given to the borrower and interest accrues year after year until the loan becomes due and payable.

Reverse mortgages are designed for those in their senior years who are "house rich" but maybe "cash poor." If someone has a lot of equity in the home and wants to tap into that equity, it typically means getting an equity loan or a cash-out refinance loan. Either way, the loan will immediately have monthly payments that must be paid.

And if the borrowers suddenly can't make the payments for whatever reason, the loan could go into foreclosure and the owners would lose their home in its entirety.

With a reverse mortgage, that would never happen. Homeowners keep their home, aren't transferring ownership to anyone, and only pay back the lender at a later date. Even if the final loan balance owed to the lender is more than the appraised value of the property at the time of loan settlement.

For instance, say a borrower took out a $100,000 reverse mortgage to retire on. Interest accrues at, say, 5.00 percent each year for several years. Recall that the loan amount is partially determined by actuary tables that include the age of the borrower at the time the loan was taken out. Let's also say that the appraised value of the property came out to be $250,000. But let's say grandpa lives a lot longer than the lender thought he would. A lot longer—so much so that the 5.00 percent interest accrual ultimately winds up being more than the appraised value of the property at the time of grandpa's demise. The loan balance might be $275,000 and the appraised value came in at $200,000.

Do the heirs owe the difference between what was ultimately accrued and what was originally calculated? Nope. If grandpa lived longer than anyone could have imagined, there is no additional amounts that need to be paid, regardless of the value of the property.

Who Qualifies for a Reverse Mortgage?

First, it's designed for seniors. The minimum age for someone to qualify for a reverse mortgage is 62. Second, the borrower must occupy and own the home either without any loans on it or, if there is a current mortgage on the property, the current loan must first be paid off before any cash proceeds can be delivered to the homeowner. How much can someone qualify for? There are actuary tables that help determine this amount, but typically, the age the person is when applying for the loan and the amount of equity in the home dictate how much cash can be had with a reverse mortgage loan.

For instance, say a borrower is 63 years old and the home is worth $200,000. With an FHA reverse mortgage, the amount the borrower could receive is about $600 a month:

Lump sum	$106,000
Line of credit	$106,000
Monthly payment	$ 600

Now, say the borrower is 75 years old and the home is worth the very same $200,000.

Lump sum	$129,000
Line of credit	$129,000
Monthly payment	$855

Finally, let's compare that same borrower at 75 years old who has a home valued at $500,000.

Lump sum	$336,000
Line of credit	$336,000
Monthly payment	$ 2,200

There is a maximum FHA reverse mortgage limit and it is set at $417,000 (the same as conventional loan limits) and $625,000 for high cost areas that include Hawaii, Alaska, Guam, and the Virgin Islands.

Would You Qualify for More with a Reverse Mortgage?

This new loan limit is quite a difference compared to just a few short years ago, when the FHA reverse limits were based on a percentage of the median family home price for the area in which the home is located. For instance, a forward FHA loan limit might be $200,000 for an Oklahoma county, but a reverse mortgage limit would be $417,000.

How Much Do Reverse Mortgages Cost?

A criticism of reverse mortgages has always been the costs associated with these types of loans. And the criticism was warranted. They are less than they were, but still pricey.

Closing costs on reverse mortgages would include the FHA mortgage insurance premium, a 2 percent origination fee in addition to the standard closing costs associated with any home loan. On a $200,000 FHA reverse mortgage, the closing costs could add up to $8,000 or more. But changes to FHA closing costs reduce the origination fee to 1 percent of the loan amount instead of 2 percent, and a flat 2 percent MIP premium is deducted from the loan proceeds. Not a big change, but a welcome change nonetheless.

How Can You Buy a New Home with a Reverse Mortgage?

Perhaps the biggest change for reverse mortgages is now the loan program can be used to purchase a new home instead of simply pulling equity out of the current property. How does that work? A borrower takes out a reverse mortgage on the current property, and then finds a new property and transfers that reverse mortgage to the new property!

This is a huge change that allows the homeowner to buy a new primary residence using equity from a current residence without having to sell the home or take out an equity loan the buyer would have to pay back for funds to buy the new home.

This is perfect for retirees who have lots of equity, or just enough, to buy a new home without all the hassles and associated costs of selling their current property first. Sometimes when people have a home to be sold, they can't qualify for the new loan because their current home hasn't sold. With the new reverse purchase program, they don't have to sell anything, just transfer the equity.

THE OTHER ZERO-DOWN-PAYMENT LOAN: USDA

This sounds a bit odd—the United States Department of Agriculture, or USDA, sponsoring a loan program—but in reality, this program has been around for literally decades. Specifically, it's Section 502 of the Rural Development Housing and Community and Facilities Program, but for everyone else it's simply the USDA loan. It's considered a major change in the mortgage world simply because of its resurgence.

This loan program has been known by other names in the past, such as the Farmers Home Administration, Farmer Mae, Rural Development loan, and others, but since the program was transferred to the USDA a few years ago, the USDA moniker has stuck. And just in the past few years, its popularity has skyrocketed.

The USDA loan program is the only other government program besides the VA home loan that requires zero down payment from the buyers, and the buyers can roll closing costs into the loan. This makes it extremely attractive for potential borrowers who qualify for the USDA loan.

Like the FHA loan, one doesn't have to be in a specific class of borrowers such as a veteran or member of the National Guard or be a first time homebuyer, but does have certain income and geographic restrictions.

With the demise of zero-down loan programs from conventional lenders, as well as the absence of alternative and subprime mortgage loans, the USDA program has gained considerable popularity as it fills a niche that the alternative loan market had occupied for years.

USDA loans can be issued directly from the government via a Federal Land Bank or through the "guaranteed" program, where the lender underwrites and funds the USDA loan using USDA guidelines and then sells the loan or services the loan themselves, as with any other mortgage.

Borrowers can qualify if their monthly gross household income does not exceed 115 percent of the median income for the area. There are also exceptions with regard to income based on the number of people in the household. These income limitations are designated by area and can be found at http://eligibility.sc.egov.usda.gov.

There are also geographic limitations, and since this is a Rural Development program, one would guess that the property must be located out in the country somewhere. Although this is certainly the case, the true definition of *rural* can be any unincorporated town or an incorporated town with less than 25,000 in population.

That's a lot more places than you would think, and even urban and suburban areas can have pockets of qualified areas where USDA loans can be placed. To locate property eligibility based on location, go to the same website at http://eligibility.sc.egov.usda.gov/eligibility. Finally, there are loan limits that must be met as well.

Once it has been determined that the buyers as well as the property conform to the USDA program, then it's on to the next step: getting approved for the mortgage.

USDA loans do not have minimum credit score requirements, nor do lenders require a minimum score, such as with other government-backed home loans. USDA simply asks that the loan application be submitted to the USDA automated underwriting system and obtain an approval. If the system approves the mortgage, then the loan continues to the remaining approval procedures. USDA loans require debt ratios and use the same ratios FHA uses, with a 29 percent housing ratio and a 41 percent total debt ratio.

USDA Loans Have Guarantee Fees

There is no monthly mortgage insurance premium (MIP) with a USDA loan, but there is a 2.00 percent "guarantee" fee, similar to the VA loan programs' funding fee. This fee can also be rolled into the loan amount as long as the total loan does not exceed 102 percent of the sales price.

For a home that sold for $100,000, the 2.00 percent guarantee fee would be $2,000, and if the buyers put zero down, then the maximum loan amount would be $102,000. With a 6.00 percent 30-year fixed-rate loan, the monthly payment would look something like this:

Principal and interest	$ 611.54
Taxes and insurance	$100.00
Total	$ 711.54

On occasion, the appraisal on a property can come in higher than the sales price. If this is the case, then additional closing costs can be rolled into the loan as well. No other loan program allows for this.

USDA Loans Have Unique Funding

USDA does not set interest rates but lets the market (lenders) decide and compete with one another for USDA business. However, USDA loans can sometimes be higher in rate when compared to conventional, VA, and FHA market rates—but not much higher. If a conventional 30-year rate could be found at 6.00 percent, then a USDA loan might be priced at 6.50 percent.

One oddity with USDA loans is how they're funded. Recall that the secondary market allows for the buying and selling of home loans to keep liquidity in the market. USDA funds come each quarter with special appropriations from Congress and are based on previous years' demand. For example, say Congress appropriates $10,000 (this is an artificially low number used only for example purposes) to fund USDA so it can buy USDA mortgages from the lenders who made them. The funds are issued each year when Congress passes its annual budget. If there is a shortfall, then Congress typically makes an emergency appropriation the following quarter to provide adequate funds.

If USDA is allotted $10,000 and at the end of the year there's still money left over, then Congress might reduce the allotted amount or leave it the same. If USDA is allotted $10,000 and the funds run out after 60 days, then Congress needs to come up with some money and fast to refund the program.

The budget for the following year would appropriate the amount of funds based on the previous years' performance. Sometimes funds are no longer available because the money is all gone and USDA has to wait for Congress to act. This doesn't happen very often, but it does happen.

NEW CHANGES TO GOVERNMENT-BACKED BOND LOAN PROGRAMS

Government can also assist with homeownership in the form of grants or loans that are backed by federal bond programs, sometimes simply called *bond loans.*

These programs are typically targeted toward first-time homebuyers although there are certainly instances where being a first-time homebuyer isn't a requirement. However, most programs do require that first-time status in order to qualify.

Exactly what is a bond program? The government can issue bonds to investors that are designed to supplement another loan program by subsidizing the interest rate issued by a conventional or government lender. Most often, these programs are issued by the state or county where the buyer is purchasing the home but are funded by federal dollars.

If a buyer qualifies for a bond loan, the buyer would apply for a mortgage at a mortgage company for a government-backed loan such as a VA loan, FHA, or USDA loan program. Some bond programs don't require the loan be government-backed and can apply to a conventional loan, but those programs are less common.

A bond loan is used to subsidize, or "buy down" the interest rate to a rate that is below current markets. Proceeds from these federal bond sales are used to offset the difference in market rate and the subsidized rate. For example, say a first-time homebuyer qualifies for a bond program offered by the state of Illinois. Current market rates for a standard FHA 30-year loan program might be 6.25 percent. The bond program has funds that reduce that mortgage rate to, say, 4.75 percent! The homebuyer applies for both the FHA loan as well as the bond program. The lender underwrites the mortgage application as if it were any other FHA loan at 6.25 percent.

After the loan is approved at the lender, the bond application is packaged with the original approval and forwarded to the lender's bond department set aside to administer these bond loans. The bond department underwrites the loan a second time to make sure it qualifies for the bond program being applied for. If it does, then the lender will issue the loan at the 4.75 percent rate, while at the same time applying for funds from the government that offset the difference in monthly payments.

Say the loan application is for a $200,000 FHA loan at 6.25 percent. With a 30-year loan, the principal and interest payment would be about $1,231 per month, while the 4.75 rate would result in a $1,043 payment, or a difference of around $188! As mentioned, these programs normally target a specific class of buyers, most often first-time homebuyers. Additional programs are often available for the following:

> - Policemen
> - Firefighters
> - Educators
> - Emergency workers
> - Other public servants

Not all lenders participate in these programs, so you'll need to do some homework upfront to make sure that the bond program is available and the lender you've selected participates in the program.

SUMMARY

- ➢ The government does not make VA or FHA loans, only guarantees them to lenders should the loans default. The government can make USDA loans directly, but most are still made by lenders and backed by the government.
- ➢ The VA does not have a minimum credit score requirement but lenders may place their own score requirements on VA loans.
- ➢ VA loans underwritten manually pay strict attention to debt ratio limits.
- ➢ New changes to VA loan limits match those of Fannie and Freddie.
- ➢ There is a new way to use the VA loan for jumbo properties.
- ➢ New method of assigning VA closing costs is on par with conventionals.
- ➢ FHA MIP refunds have been eliminated except in FHA refinances.
- ➢ The government no longer participates in seller-assisted downpayment programs.
- ➢ FHA closing costs are on par with conventional loans.
- ➢ FHA lenders all require minimum credit scores.
- ➢ FHA is now the only source for reverse mortgages with changes to loan limits, reduced closing fees, and can now be used to purchase a home as well.
- ➢ USDA has been identified as a new source for zero-down loans.
- ➢ Government bond and grant programs have emerged.

Qualifying the New Way: Understanding Automated Underwriting Systems

UNDERWRITERS ARE individuals who are highly regarded in the mortgage business, and those underwriters who have been in the business for a long time have earned their way to the top and can make a very good income. Some underwriters even obtain a special status that authorizes them to underwrite certain types of loans that other underwriters aren't qualified to fully approve.

There are several factors that a loan application must pass muster on before an approval is issued but they fall into two basic categories: property and borrowers. We will discuss these, before moving on to the details of the automated underwriting system.

PROPERTY

The property is one of the two main considerations when seeking a loan approval. Even if the borrower had perfect credit with 50 percent down and single-digit debt ratios, if the property didn't pass muster with the lender, it wouldn't matter how strong the borrower was.

Does the lender like one type of property and not like another type? Is it easier to get a loan for a three-bedroom brick home than it is for a two-bedroom condominium? Are duplexes more desirable because they can generate income through rentals?

Lenders don't prefer one property type over another, but what they do like to see is that the property in question doesn't stick out like a sore thumb in the neighborhood. In other words, are there similar properties nearby or down the street that have recently sold? Is the subject property a single-family residence? Is it a townhouse? Are there other single-family residences or townhouses? Such similar properties are called "comparable sales" or simply "comps." Conventional as well as government loans require that there be other properties in the area that would be considered equivalent property types. This is, after all, the lenders' collateral, and marketability of the property is essential.

New Changes to Appraisals Mean More Work, More Money

Specifically, such guidelines ask that there be at least three other properties in the area, ideally within one mile of the subject property, that have sold within the previous 12 months. Why is that important to a lender?

Recall that the secondary market, which buys and sells mortgage loans, likes loans that are similar in nature. That includes the property type. If there are three other similar properties that have sold within a one-mile radius, then the property would be considered "normal" or "standard" for the area.

Lenders need to view the property in such a light to prepare for a worst-case scenario; should the lender ever have to foreclose on the property due to nonpayment, would the lender have a property that is similar to other properties, or would it have on its hands a white elephant that would take forever to sell due to some unique set of characteristics?

For instance, the seller of a property had a penchant for geodesic domes, so he built one right smack in the middle of Normalsville, USA. He might be able to find a buyer who also has fallen in love with geodesic domes who has more than 20 percent down, great credit, and sufficient income to qualify for a mortgage.

If it's the only geodesic dome in the neighborhood, there will be no mortgage loan. The property wouldn't have any comps. No other geodesic domes, no mortgage. By contrast, if the property in question is a three-bedroom, two-bath brick home, it's likely that other homes in the area are similar, with perhaps some two-bedroom and four-bedroom homes of similar size. Then the property would be acceptable to the lender.

It's the appraiser who establishes for the lender the marketability of the property, both in terms of comps and sales price.

The availability of comps is a key element of marketability. But what if there are no comps within one mile of the subject? If that's the case, then lenders will accept an explanation of the market that while there are comparable sales, there aren't very many of them due to the size of the neighborhood or the town where the property is located. As long as the case is made that the property does, in fact, have comps, and even though the comps are outside the one-mile radius, then a lender would still consider the loan.

The other piece of the marketability puzzle is to justify the price of the home. Say there's a three-bedroom home for sale at $300,000. The home has been on the market for a couple of months when finally an offer is accepted at $280,000. The lender engages an appraiser to appraise the property. As part of the appraiser's research, the appraiser is provided a copy of the executed sales contract. It is in this way that the appraiser attempts to justify the sales price agreed to for the property. Sales contract in hand, the appraiser does some research by accessing the local multiple listing service, a database for real estate that is currently listed or recently sold, to see if there are other properties in the area that are within one mile of the subject and sold within the previous 12 months.

The appraiser will make note of the potential comps and visit each one, along with visiting the subject property. The appraisal itself is a narrative with pictures of both the subject property and the comps.

The appraiser will compare all the properties, using things such as square footage, number of bedrooms, number of bathrooms, the size of the lot, and so on. The appraiser will then review the sales prices of the comps and compare them to the subject.

Generally speaking, if a home sold for $300,000 and is 3,000 square feet, then the house sold for $100 per square foot. If the subject home is 2,800 square feet and sold for $280,000, then the subject home sold for $100 per square foot.

The appraiser will do the very same thing with the other comps to see if the price per square foot method seems to fit the other houses as well. If all the other recent comps sold for somewhere around $100 per square foot, then it's likely the sales price of the subject property is within range of other local sales. If a property in the neighborhood sold for much less than that, say $80 per foot on a 2,800 square foot home, or $224,000, then there will be some more research needed to adjust for the lower price per square foot.

These "adjustments" vary, and there can be some subjectivity to them. For instance, one home might have a swimming pool that was installed for $25,000. That won't necessarily add $25,000 to the value of a home. Some people don't want a swimming pool in their backyard. Perhaps the kitchen has been significantly updated with granite countertops and top-of-the-line appliances. Updated kitchens can add value to almost any home.

Still more, one property might be sitting on a hilltop and have a nice view of the valley below from the living room, while the other comparable sales are down the hill with no view whatsoever. The value of the home at the top of the hill will be adjusted upward to account for the superior view the property enjoys compared to the other properties.

Once the appraiser has visited all the properties and accounted for their adjustments, the appraiser will determine whether the subject property supports the value listed in the sales contract.

Most often, that is the case. A "market value" means the amount on the sales contract that represents the highest price the buyer was willing to pay compared to the lowest price the seller was willing to accept, all things being equal.

All things being equal means the offer and acceptance were made without duress under the very same market conditions. For instance, the seller of the property had to sell quickly or be foreclosed on, thus lowering the price to attract a quick offer. In a stable market, the sales contract and the appraisal almost always agree.

Still another new change in appraisal guidelines is an addition to the appraisal report itself. This addition is called the *market conditions report*. In addition to finding previous sales, new changes require more stringent guidelines.

Without knowing about these guidelines in advance, you could find yourself making an offer on a home and the appraisal not coming in at the proper valuation. Say that you made an offer on a home for $300,000 and the appraisal report came back with a valuation of only $280,000. This presents a significant problem.

Lenders base loan amounts and down payment requirements on the lower of the sales price or appraised value. In this example, the loan would be based on $280,000 and not $300,000. If the lender requires 5 percent down on the loan, the 5 percent would be based on $280,000.

If the seller stands firm and demands the sales price hold at $300,000 then the buyer must make up the difference. Instead of coming into the closing with 5 percent of $300,000, or $15,000, the buyer must now come in with 5 percent of $280,000 plus $20,000, representing the difference between $300,000 and $280,000.

Declining Market Means More Down Payment

The new changes require the market conditions report, which describes the local real estate market in its current condition. This report will help to identify what is called a *declining market*. A declining market is a local real estate market where real estate values have been declining consistently over the previous 12-month period.

When an appraiser does the research and finds that home values have declined, the appraiser must complete the report as well as make an indication on the appraisal report itself identifying the local market as "declining."

In a declining market, a lender will require another 5 percent down, regardless of the original loan approval. Again, using the same $300,000 sales price with 5 percent down, if the market is identified as declining, then the lender will require 10 percent down and not 5 percent. That's another $15,000.

You should use your agent or someone such as an appraiser who can help with identifying current market values, because it could affect the ability to get your loan approved. Remember, it's not just you and your credit that get approved, but the property as well.

In addition to finding at least three sales in the previous 12 months, the appraiser must also find a minimum of two comps that are within three months of the appraisal date. In addition, at least two active listings must be in the report. A *listing* is a home that is for sale on the market but hasn't yet sold. This is a significant departure from previous appraisal requirements, because a listing may or may not sell for the advertised price. Often, the list price is open for negotiations between the seller and the buyer.

The appraiser must also use current sales and listing data to reflect what is called a *list to sales price ratio*. This ratio shows the difference between the original list price and what it finally sold for. The report must also research any changes in list prices while the home is being listed for sale.

For instance, the home could have originally been on the market for six months at $300,000 with no offers. Then the seller dropped the list price to, say, $290,000. The appraiser must report that price change.

Watch Out: Too Many Seller Concessions Can Lower Your Value

Finally, the appraiser will research the market to see if the current sales offered any seller concessions. On closed comparable sales, the appraiser can determine whether or not the seller of the property agreed to pay some closing costs on behalf of the buyer. For example, the buyer and seller could agree on a $300,000 sales price, but the seller agrees to pay $3,000 in buyer closing costs.

On a closed sale, that seller concession is reported on the appraisal form. The new requirements mean the appraiser must note any *pending sales*—sales that are in the process of closing but not yet closed—that have any sort of seller concessions in the contract. If it is determined that the seller gave up too much in the form of seller concessions, the lender just might deduct that amount from the appraised value. When seller concessions exceed 4 percent of the sales price, be prepared to see your value reduced. That means coming into the closing with more down payment money.

All of this requires extra work on behalf of the appraiser, and sometimes not all of this information is available. Perhaps the appraisal asks for two recent sales within 90 days of the appraisal date and there are none. In the instance where the lender requires information that simply isn't available, the appraiser will be asked to address that fact in a written report.

These additional changes help the lending industry when evaluating appraised values when compared to contracts, but it also means appraisers now charge more for their services. These additional reporting requirements can add another $100 to a standard $350 appraisal.

Title Issues: It Has to Be Yours

Another important consideration regarding the property identifies any current legal interests in the property itself, any previous liens that haven't been released, or any personal judgments against the owner of the property that may lay claim to the real estate.

A title report is a report that gives a historical record of any previous ownership in the property. If Joe originally owned the property and later sold it to Sally, who later sold it to Bob, who later sold it to Tim, then this "chain of title" would serve as a record of not just who owned it, but that ownership legally changed hands from one party to the next.

When Joe sold the property to Sally, the sale would be legally recorded as a public document where Joe gives up all interests in the property and transfers the real estate to Sally, usually as a result of selling the property. A title report will make certain that the property legally changed hands and Joe had no more legal claims to the property. The same would be recorded when Sally sold the property to Bob, and so on.

Sometimes property transfers don't completely release the property into a buyer's hands. A common instance might be that Joe was originally married and his ex-wife owned part of the real estate but didn't relinquish her interest in the property to Sally. Or there might be a previous lien that was recorded on the property but never released. A roofing contractor may have done some roof work and filed a mechanic's lien on the property while the work was being performed. Such liens are commonly filed during any work on real estate to ensure the contractor gets paid. Once the contractor gets paid for work performed, the contractor releases the lien.

Sometimes, the contractor and the property owner disagree—for instance, on whether or not the job was completed satisfactorily—and the homeowner refuses to pay. The lien remains on the property until at such the time property is sold or transferred to another party. If there is a previously recorded lien on Joe's property that hasn't been released, then the lien will have to be paid before Joe can sell the property to Sally, who will then be recorded as the legal owner.

Other issues with title can result in a lawsuit or damages awarded to someone if there is a judgment levied by the court on the owner of the property. If Sally got into a lawsuit and lost, then the winner of that suit might place a lien on her house until she paid the settlement.

If the title report comes in "clean" meaning there are no previous unsettled claims or illegal transfers of ownership, the lender will determine that the property is eligible to make a loan against it.

BORROWERS

We reviewed borrower characteristics in the previous two chapters with regards to credit, income, and assets, but underwriters now need to know more about all three other than what appears at face value.

You Must Have Established Credit

We discussed how credit is established and the items that make up a credit report in Chapter 2, and we'll discuss how to repair credit in Chapter 8.

Big Changes: All Income Must Be Verified

One big change is that all income must be verified. At first glance, this might sound obvious, but for years, when an automated underwriting system would evaluate a loan application, sometimes it wouldn't require the lender to verify that you make what you said you made on your loan application. Experienced loan officers could review a loan application and credit report and tell whether income documentation was required. In many instances, not even a pay stub would be needed, and there was only a phone call to the employer to see if the applicant was still employed. Not anymore. Income documentation is now a part of every single loan file.

Income is used to calculate debt ratios and each program can have its own maximum debt ratio. But exactly what type of income is available, and how is it calculated?

The first requirement is that the income must be derived from full-time employment. We'll discuss how part-time income can be used later in this chapter. Full time typically means at minimum 36 hours of work each week for those who get paid hourly. They work for someone else and get paid on a regular basis.

This is the easiest type of income to verify, as the verification of the income is stated on the W-2 issued by the federal government and can be matched up using pay stubs. If the W-2 says the borrower makes $24,000 per year and the borrowers pay stub reflects $2,000 per month in gross income, then the income can then be verified. *Verified* means documented by a third party, in this case the employer and the federal government.

This verification method works for both salaried as well as hourly employees. For those paid by the hour, the underwriter reviews the W-2 as well as the most recent pay stubs covering 30 days.

The pay stub will reflect how many hours were worked during the pay period (remember, a minimum of 36 hours counts as full time), as well as the hourly pay rate. If the borrower made $12.00 per hour and worked 80 hours for a two-week period, the underwriter would figure out the borrower worked 40 hours per week at $12.00 per hour, or $480 per week. The underwriter would multiply $480 times 52 (weeks) to get $24,960, then divide that amount by 12 (months). The result is $2,080 gross income per month.

Debt ratios use gross monthly income, but what if someone gets paid every other week and not twice per month? Careful now—there is a difference. Each month doesn't contain exactly four weeks. February does in a non–leap year, but that's it.

To calculate the income for someone who gets paid every other week, take the gross pay for that pay period and multiply that by 26, the number of pay periods per year for those who get paid every other week. That's 52 weeks divided by two.

If someone makes $4,000 every other week, then she would make $8,667 per month. That's $4,000 times 26 weeks divided by 12.

What about that hourly employee who works overtime; how are those numbers calculated? In order for an underwriter to use overtime as regular income, the overtime must be proven to be consistent. Consistent means having a two-year history of overtime, as well as a letter from the employer stating overtime is likely to continue.

This is sometimes hard to satisfy. Employers can be reluctant to put anything in writing with regards to future overtime, but an underwriter can make the determination by reviewing pay stubs and previous years W-2 information.

Part-Time Changes: Same Line of Work and One Employer

Part-time income can also be a challenge. Part-time income must also show a two-year history of part-time work and, of course, still be employed in the part-time position. Even if there is a history of part-time employment, it must now be part-time employment in the same line of work. Further, many lenders won't accept part-time income from separate employers, regardless of there being a two-year history.

Those are the easy income calculations. An underwriter will manually calculate gross monthly income from these sources. But what if you are self-employed?

Old Underwriting Requirement Returns to Haunt the Self-Employed

Without a doubt, the biggest change for those who are self-employed is how long they need to be self-employed in order to count their income. First and foremost, you must be self-employed for at least two years, as verified by income tax returns.

There were other ways lenders could use self-employment income, as long as income from the previous six months could be established, but that guideline went away and an old one returned; two years of tax returns.

Notice that doesn't mean two years self-employment, it means two years of tax returns showing self-employment income. The distinction between the two works like this; say you started a business in October of 2008. Eighteen months later would be April 2010 and likely you've filed two years of tax returns, one for 2008 and one for 2009. You've just met the income requirements for the self-employed by evidence of two years' worth of returns. But you haven't met the requirement to be self-employed for two years. For that, you'll have to wait until October 2010

You'll need to show at least some minimal income for your business for the year 2008, even if it was only a few hundred dollars. But once you've filed tax returns for 2008 and 2009 and business income is shown for tax years 2008 and 2009, you're good to go. Once you've met both requirements, you can use your self-employed income.

Assets Can Be Liquid or Nonliquid

Assets are the third leg of the stool. In addition to having established credit and verifying income, underwriters will confirm the assets that are used for down payment when needed and for closing costs. Assets are funds brought to the closing table, most often in the form of a cashier's check.

Assets can be money in the bank or in the stock market or in a retirement account. Liquid assets are funds you can access relatively quickly. Money in the bank or cashing in some stock is a liquid account. Money in retirement funds such as a 401(k) or IRA is considered nonliquid.

Lenders sometimes utilize an underwriting guideline called "reserves" in addition to funds needed for down payment and closing costs. Most often, lenders require these reserves for low-down-payment mortgages to bolster the overall file.

Reserves are typically defined in terms of months of house payments. If a lender requires six months' worth of reserves and the house payment is $2,000 per month, then the loan approval will require $12,000 in additional assets beyond down payment and closing cost money. A nonliquid account would be used as part of the reserve asset, but not all of it. A lender can use 80 percent of the current value of the nonliquid account as reserves. This percent is used to estimate any early withdrawal penalties the borrower might incur should those reserve funds be accessed for any reason. Except if you're a first time homebuyer.

 First-timers beware: There are changes in reserve requirements.

Lenders as well as mortgage insurance companies can require reserves, but if you're a first-time homebuyer, neither will typically allow nonliquid funds to be counted as reserves. Especially with less than 20 percent down. If they are putting less than 20 percent down, first-timers take it on the chin two more times—once from the mortgage insurance company who won't count reserves for first timers and second from the lien lenders, who may not count nonliquid assets, either. This is a little-known change that can have a huge impact on those buying their first home.

AUTOMATED UNDERWRITING SYSTEMS

An underwriter may manually review all aspects of the loan application, but this is unusual. For obvious reasons, this process is called *manual underwriting*. It's performed by hand and can take hours. But manual underwriting has all but disappeared. It used to be an option, but nowadays, lenders don't like to manually underwrite loans. Loans are now approved using an automated underwriting system, or AUS.

During a manual underwrite, the underwriter literally evaluates the entire file, doing what an automated system can do in mere seconds. When a human makes any number of calculations, as underwriters do when evaluating a loan request, the possibility for mistakes is increased. If a mistake is made on a loan file and the loan goes bad, the loan has to be bought back by the original lender as described in the first chapter.

Make Sure Your Loan Application Is Ready for Automated Underwriting

Automated underwriting systems came about during the late 1990s and were used primarily for conventional loans. Instead of a human underwriter making a loan decision, a loan application is converted electronically then submitted to the AUS. Within a few moments, the approval is issued, along with a list of conditions—much like an underwriter would review a loan manually, but in reverse.

Instead of manually approving a loan with a list of conditions to come after the underwrite, the file is submitted electronically to obtain the list of conditions. Only after the loan has been submitted to the AUS will the file begin to be documented. This is done to see if the loan itself is eligible for approval, and if it isn't, then the loan will either be declined or the lender will determine whether the loan has enough merit to be approved with the skills of a human underwriter.

Lenders don't like that sort of risk. If a loan doesn't get approved with an AUS and the lender decides to go ahead and approve it anyway, the lender will either have to keep the loan or hope it can sell the loan on the secondary market.

If a loan doesn't get an automated approval, then it's much less likely the loan could be sold. And if the loan did get approved with a manual underwrite and the loan in fact was sold, if the loan ever went bad, the original lender would be required to buy the loan back from the entity it first sold it to. Lenders don't like such a potential albatross and rely on an AUS as a quality control mechanism to ensure the loan meets secondary guidelines.

When loan officers take a loan application, they run the application to check for errors and then submit the application to an AUS. Each loan type has its own automated underwriting system. Fannie Mae has the Desktop Underwriter and Desktop Originator, Freddie Mac uses Loan Prospector, FHA has the Scorecard, and VA and USDA use GUS, or government underwriting system.

In reality, these are all nearly identical in practice, with a few tweaks to adhere more closely to whichever type loan is being applied for. A VA AUS will make allowances for zero money down; FHA requires a minimum 3.5 percent down, for instance.

Loan officers can submit the application even though there is no property picked out. This is important for buyers who want their approval in their hands before they go house hunting. For instance, the buyers' debt ratios might be high or the credit is shaky. Having the loan submitted through an AUS before shopping can put those fears to rest.

The AUS can also be used in order to tweak the loan application to get an approval. A loan that gets an approval from an AUS may not have a debt ratio requirement. Say that a buyer has a debt ratio of 52, much higher than a typical 38 ratio, and is not sure if the buyer could get approved.

In the past, an underwriter who performed a manual underwrite would likely decline the mortgage application due to such high ratios. But as long as an approval is issued with an AUS, it doesn't matter what the ratios are to still have a loan that's eligible for sale on the secondary market.

An AUS is a time saver for both the borrower and the lender. Historically, a loan officer would ask for nearly everything under the sun when taking a loan application. This means asking for anything that might possibly come up during the loan approval process. A typical request would be:

- Two years tax returns
- Two years W-2s
- Two months most recent pay stubs
- Year to date profit and loss statement
- Three months of the most recent bank and investment statements
- Name and contact information for homeowners insurance
- Copy of divorce decree, if applicable
- Letters of explanation for derogatory credit
- Letters of explanation for gaps in employment

All of this would be asked for before an underwriter ever saw the loan. Just in case it was needed. The file would be further documented by ordering all the legal and title work, plus the appraisal. Then the borrowers would wait to see if their loan was approved or not approved. That could take a couple of weeks or more, taking up precious time.

The AUS turns all that upside down. The loan application is run through the AUS and the decision comes back with a list of only the things needed to make the loan eligible for sale on the secondary market. It complies with conventional or government guidelines. After the loan has gone through the AUS, the list of documentation would then read something like this:

- One most recent pay stub
- Verbal verification of employment

➤ One most recent bank statement

➤ Evidence of insurance coverage

Notice that the list is much smaller. It can be much smaller because the AUS only asks for the things required to close the loan; no more and no less. The AUS will automatically review credit scores, sufficient funds available for closing, and debt-to-income ratios. All within a matter of moments.

Automated Double-Check: Note the Changes in the Automated Process

Lenders discovered that even loans with automated approvals can require additional work. These new changes took place primarily in two areas: mortgage insurance for loans with less than 20 percent down and income verification.

As mortgage insurance companies found themselves with insurance settlements they had to pay on loans that got approved with automated underwriting, they decided to take matters into their own hands. We'll discuss in more detail these mortgage insurance changes later in this chapter, but mortgage insurance companies quit insuring conventional loans with less than 5 percent down, effectively eliminating Fannie and Freddie's 3 percent down-payment, first-time homebuyer programs called "Home Possible" and "My Community."

The next big change in double-checking an automated underwriting decision regarded verifying income. An AUS would ask the lender to verify the pay by a pay stub and a W-2, for instance, but lenders now take it a step further by requesting directly from the IRS the borrowers' tax returns and W-2s for the previous two years—even if it was not required by the AUS, and even if the borrowers provided those items directly to the lender.

Historically, all borrowers would sign the IRS form 4506 with each initial loan application. This form would allow lenders to pull previous years tax returns to compare the income reported to the IRS to what was reported on the application. But this was only done in rare cases during a routine loan audit or the loan went into foreclosure.

Now, however, this is a huge change—the borrowers sign the IRS form 4506-T at application. During the approval process, the lender takes this form and obtains the previous two years of tax returns, W-2s, 1099s, and any other schedules the borrower may have filed. This is done electronically and takes only a day or two. When the tax information is received, the lender manually compares the income with what the IRS reported to the lender with what the applicants reported to the lender.

With the proper software, applicants can provide fake tax returns and even fake W-2s, but if they do that now, the loan will never make it past the underwriting stage. The applicants have just committed loan fraud and the lender has proof. The loan will be denied.

Get to Yes with an AUS

The AUS approval, then, is not automatic. Sometimes the loan is not approved. If that is the case, then the lender would make the determination of whether to manually override the AUS decision and underwrite the loan themselves without an AUS decision (highly doubtful) or the loan officer needs to adjust certain things on the loan application itself. When an AUS declines a loan application, the reason(s) for the declination will be listed on the AUS report in order of importance.

Recall that the AUS won't have a maximum debt ratio but looks at the entire application at once to reach a decision. Let's say that the borrower had a debt ratio that was 55. That's high, but because of the good credit, the loan officer decided to try for the approval anyway.

So the loan officer submits the file to the AUS and gets a decline. The reason might read something like this:

➤ Debt to income ratios high

➤ Minimal down payment used

These reasons for declination could then be addressed and run again. If the debt-to-income ratios are too high, then try putting more money down. That strategy would address both declination reasons—ratios too high and minimal amount down. The loan officer would then massage the loan application, and instead of putting 5 percent down, the loan officer would enter 10 percent down and resubmit the application to the AUS.

The AUS could return with an approval and the borrowers would go about documenting their file per the AUS request. But what if the borrower doesn't have additional funds to put down?

If the file is resubmitted through an AUS, the file must be documented in the exact same fashion as the new approval was issued. In this example, the borrowers must find some more down payment money, either by saving it up or getting a gift from a family member. We'll explore unique sources of down payment and closing cost funds in detail in Chapter 7.

Change the Terms

Another way to change a decline into an acceptance is to reduce the monthly payment by taking a lower rate or extending the loan term. If the ratio was at 55 with an interest rate of 6.00 percent, then try submitting the application to the AUS yet again with a rate of 5.75 percent, lowering the payment, which lowers the debt ratio.

Longer-term mortgages, say a 30-year loan compared to a 15-year loan, will have lower monthly payments. Most lenders allow for loans to be amortized, or stretched out, over 40 years. So if a 30-year loan gets declined due to ratios, ask the lender to try the submission with a 40-year term.

Perhaps there are some debts that can be paid off. An AUS will consider an installment loan paid off completely, as long as there are less than 10 months remaining on the account. This is most common with an automobile loan.

Change Your Ratios

Let's look at the 55 debt ratio problem again. If the loan is declined due to ratios, examine your credit report to see if there are any installment accounts that you can pay down below 10 months remaining.

Say your car payment is $500 per month and there is a $6,000 balance. That's 12 months left, and the AUS would count that as a debt. But your loan officer can resubmit the application showing nine months remaining to see if you can get your approval. If your choices are to reduce ratios but you don't want to or can't come up with more down payment money to do so, then try reducing your loan balances by paying them down—but not completely, if you don't want to.

Instead of coming up with an additional $15,000, or 5 percent on a $300,000 home, simply pay your car loan down by $1,500 so you have less than 10 months remaining.

Such scenarios can be run over and over again to try and obtain an approval. Note that resubmitting doesn't mean trying to falsify your income. If you're declined due to high ratios, you can't simply enter more income on your application if you don't have it. Lying on an application is fraud. Remember that the lender will verify the income at some point so you're wasting your time.

AUS Approval: What It Says Is What You Do

After you receive your AUS approval and have complied with the documentation request, the loan is then sent to the underwriter for approval. But instead of calculating debt ratios, evaluating credit and reviewing bank statements, the underwriter simply goes down the list of required items to make sure the documentation matches up with the AUS approval.

An AUS approval could say, "Minimum investment $18,780,"

and the underwriter would simply look at the bank statement to see whether there was a $18,780 balance. If there wasn't, the underwriter would ask to see more funds either deposited into the account or saved up.

Or the approval would read, "Verify income of $5,000 per month," and the underwriter would look at the pay stub to see if the borrower makes $5,000 per month. There is no need to calculate debt ratios, as the AUS decision has already performed that task. The underwriter simply makes sure the income is there and can be used as qualifying income.

The AUS works the very same way for a refinance as for a purchase loan. But instead of a sales contract establishing the value of the home, the homeowner makes a determination of the approximate value of the real estate. During a refinance application, the homeowner would say something like, "I'm applying for a $300,000 loan and I think my house is worth $500,000," and the loan officer would input that information for the AUS.

You'll notice that I mentioned how your loan officer or lender can resubmit your application after tweaking the application. Or that your loan officer or lender would submit your loan application to an AUS immediately upon receiving your application.

I'll put it another way. Your loan officer or lender is *supposed* to do it that way. There are loan officers who still document files the old-fashioned way who don't submit your file to an AUS until your loan is fully documented. This is foolish and can waste time as well as money. If your loan isn't approved by your contract date, then you could lose your earnest money deposit.

Ask your loan officer at the outset if your loan has been submitted to an AUS. If it has, make sure you get a list of the items the AUS is asking for. If the loan officer hasn't submitted your loan to an AUS, then have him do it immediately.

Automated underwriting is a real time saver as well as a method for lenders to ensure that the loans they approve fully meet lending guidelines and they can rest at night knowing their loans are sound. If the AUS issues an approval, traditional underwriting guidelines can be bypassed. That is, unless there's mortgage insurance involved.

PRIVATE MORTGAGE INSURANCE

Mortgage insurance has been around since the 1950s, but it's not the kind of insurance you might imagine. Sometimes when people hear the term "mortgage insurance" they think of an insurance policy that pays the mortgage if the homeowner gets sick or can't work. That's not how mortgage insurance works. It's an insurance policy all right, but it's a policy in favor of the lender, less so for the borrower.

Mortgage insurance can be called private mortgage insurance, or PMI, or can be the government brand of insurance in the form of a funding fee for VA loans, guarantee fee for USDA loans and the mortgage insurance premium, or MIP, for FHA loans.

Government insurance policies are paid by the borrower when they go to the closing table, and all government loans require it (except FHA loans that are amortized over 15 years, which do not require MIP).

Conventional loans require mortgage insurance when the loan amount is above 80 percent of the sales price or appraised value. If the value was $100,000, then if the loan was above $80,000, mortgage insurance would be required. Why have mortgage insurance at all, and why does the borrower have to pay it if the loss payee is the lender?

Recall in the first chapter how banks wouldn't make a home loan unless the buyer had 20, 30, or even 50 percent or more for down payment? If someone wanted to finance a home but the home was higher than FHA or VA limits allowed, then the buyer would have to come up with a significantly higher down payment.

Enter *private mortgage insurance,* or PMI.

PMI was first invented in 1957 by an insurance company named Mortgage Guaranty Insurance Corporation, or MGIC. The policy worked this way:

➤ If the lender required 20 percent down and the buyer had only 5 percent, MGIC would issue an insurance policy that would pay the lender an amount that worked out to approximately the difference between 5 percent down and 20 percent down.

➤ When lenders saw that they really couldn't lose in that situation, they began to allow for low-down-payment loans, as little as 3 percent or even less. MGIC would also underwrite the loan at the same time the lender underwrote the loan.

➤ MGIC would review credit and income and assets just like the lender would before issuing a mortgage insurance policy.

➤ MGIC would approve the policy, then send that insurance policy to the lender, who would include it with the loan file.

Mortgage insurance policies can vary in price, depending on the amount down and other credit factors. A mortgage insurance policy will be more expensive for someone with 5 percent down than for someone with 10 percent down because there's less risk for the insurance company.

The permutations are many, as various factors can impact the price of the insurance, including credit score, loan type, amortization period, the amount of down payment, and even the type of property being acquired, such as a duplex or a condominium.

As a general rule of thumb, however, simply multiplying the loan amount by 0.5 percent and then dividing by 12 (months) would give the monthly mortgage insurance premium.

It is figured like this: 0.5 percent of $300,000 would be $1,500, which, divided by 12, is $125. The mortgage insurance payment (MIP) would be $125 with 5 percent down. With 10 percent down, the MIP would drop to nearly half that, to $75 per month.

With a loan that required insurance, the lender would make two separate loan files, one for its own underwriter and one for the insurance company. The loan would, in essence, receive two different approvals.

Later, in the 1980s, mortgage insurance was an established business with proven risk models. So much so that mortgage insurance companies began to allow lenders to underwrite mortgage insurance policies in the same fashion as the lender approved the mortgage application. Instead of sending out a loan file to the insurance company, the lender would obtain "delegated" underwriting authority.

That simply meant the insurance company delegated the approval process for the insurance policy to the lender. If the lender approved the loan application, then the mortgage insurance policy was also automatically approved. This made the process more efficient and ultimately saved the borrower, the lender, and the insurance company money.

In the late 1990s and early 2000s, more and more loan types were introduced. Most of these subprime and alternative loans asked for less than 20 percent down, or at least didn't require 20 percent down. Since they were conventional loans with less than 20 percent down, the loans required mortgage insurance, and mortgage insurance companies developed policies for these new loan types. Lenders would introduce a new type of mortgage and send it to a mortgage insurance company to see if they would issue a mortgage insurance policy based on the new loan parameters. If the mortgage insurance company issued such a policy, then the lender was free to market the loan with little to nothing down.

Of course we all know what eventually happened. These loans began to default in large numbers, and that meant that mortgage insurance companies had to pay billions of dollars to mortgage companies in the form of an insurance payout.

Mortgage insurance companies then stopped the practice of allowing lenders to issue mortgage insurance policies if the loan itself was approved. Mortgage insurance firms across the board began to establish their own set of underwriting guidelines that had to be met in addition to any conditions the lender might issue.

This soon meant that a loan could get a loan approval but couldn't get mortgage insurance approval. If a lender can't get mortgage insurance on a loan with less than 20 percent down, the lender won't issue the loan regardless of what the AUS said. Since PMI is "private" mortgage insurance, it only applies to conventional mortgages and not government-backed loans such as VA, FHA, or USDA.

You can now get an AUS decision but still not get approved because you couldn't obtain PMI, because PMI now has underwriting guidelines of their very own. You'd have to wait to save up some more money to avoid down payment or elect to take out a second mortgage. We'll discuss second mortgages in Chapter 6.

PMI's new approval guidelines now require minimum credit scores, greater down payment requirements, restriction on property types, and debt-to-income ratio requirements.

PMI Now Has Minimum Credit Score Requirements

Perhaps one of the biggest changes in PMI is the requirement of minimum credit scores. As with mortgage loans, PMI did not used to require a minimum credit score as long as the loan was approved.

Now, however, PMI not only has a requirement for a credit score but it is more onerous than what lenders use. Lenders will ask for a credit score to be at least 620, but PMI companies demand that the score be 700 or better.

This 700 score is for purchases or refinance loans where no money is being taken out during the refinance, most often called a "rate and term" refinance. Still further, if the credit score is less than 720 but still 700 or above, the PMI policy will require at least two months of principal, interest, taxes, and insurance (PITI) in the bank for cash reserves.

This means that if the PITI (including mortgage insurance) is

$3,000, then the PMI policy will ask that $6,000 in liquid reserves be verified. Liquid reserves are cash accounts that are available after the closing takes place.

If the borrower has to put 10 percent down on a $300,000 sales price plus $5,000 in closing costs, that would mean a total outlay of $35,000. But with the two months PITI reserve requirement with a $3,000 per month PITI payment, that would require verification of not only the $35,000 for down payment and closing costs, but also $6,000 for the cash reserve fund. Cash reserves aren't given to the lender or PMI company but must be verified to exist.

There Are No More Zero-Down PMI Policies

Gone are zero-down conventional loans, and so are the PMI policies that covered them. There are 3 percent down loans from conventional lenders, but PMI policies don't cover anything with less than 5 percent down. Even if the lender has a 3 percent down loan, PMI companies may not insure the mortgage, so it makes the 3 percent down loan essentially worthless.

PMI Now Only Covers Certain Property Types

PMI policies can now only apply to a primary residence, as PMI for investment (rental) properties are no longer available.

Condominiums are also restricted to purchase mortgage loans and can't be used for a refinance loan. This impacts someone who bought a condo with 10 percent down and then two years later wanted to refinance because rates went down. Unless the value of the condo has appreciated enough that the loan no longer needs PMI, then the loan won't close.

And also forget the notion that even if the condominium owner could, in fact, use PMI for a refinance, if the refinance pulled out cash, then that's forbidden. As are PMI policies for duplexes, triplexes, and fourplexes.

PMI Now Limits Debt Ratios

Debt ratios are limited to 41 percent. This ratio includes all housing, revolving, and installment debt. Unlike conventional or government loans, where ratios are a general guideline as long as the loan receives an automated approval, the debt ratio requirement is typically nonnegotiable.

Finally, and perhaps the most striking changes with mortgage insurance, is the fact that some PMI companies no longer accept applications from third-party originators and that mortgage insurance is now tax deductible for first-time homebuyers.

PMI May Not Accept Loan Applications from Third-Party Originators

Third-party originators, or TPOs, are companies that originate a mortgage loan that are not lenders. This means mortgage brokers. We'll examine the differences between mortgage brokers and bankers in detail in Chapter 5.

PMI Is Now Tax Deductible (for Some Buyers)

Prior to 2008, mortgage insurance was not tax deductible but an added expense to a monthly mortgage payment for the privilege of not having to put 20 percent or more down to buy a house.

This feature made mortgage insurance less attractive when compared to certain other options, such as a second mortgage being placed behind a first mortgage to avoid PMI. As PMI became tax deductible, it was on an even playing field with second mortgages, because monthly payments between PMI and second loans were essentially the same and also a tax deduction.

But not for everyone. This tax deductibility feature only applies to first-time homebuyers. A first-time homebuyer is specifically defined as someone who has not owned a home in the previous three-year period. A lender can verify that fact by reviewing a credit report to see if a mortgage appeared on the credit report within the previous three years or even review personal income tax returns to see if a mortgage interest deduction was taken.

This does bring up a slight loophole in the guideline, because someone could have owned a house four years ago, sold it, and didn't own a home for the previous three years. In this sense, someone who wasn't actually a first-time buyer could, by definition, be one and qualify for tax deductibility of PMI.

SUMMARY

- Automated underwriting replaced manual underwriting methods.
- New appraisal requirements make them more thorough and more expensive to the consumer.
- Declining market indication requires buyers to put 5 percent more into the deal.
- Limits on seller concessions are in place.
- Properties must have clean history of ownership, evidenced by a title report.
- Everything in a loan application must be verified via third party.
- New rules apply to overtime and part-time income.
- Extinct underwriting rule requiring two years of tax returns for self-employed were reintroduced.
- Asset reserve requirements changed to limit the use of nonliquid accounts.
- New restrictions were placed on first-time homebuyers by lenders and mortgage insurance companies.
- Manual underwriting is mostly nonexistent.
- IRS 4506-T form is now required on all mortgage applications.
- AUS decisions can be tweaked to obtain an approval.
- Mortgage insurance companies developed their own underwriting guidelines.

Banks, Mortgage Banks, and Mortgage Brokers in the New Mortgage Market

THE HOME LOAN INDUSTRY is constantly evolving. Even though it may not seem that way on a day-to-day or even month-to-month basis, it's changing. In the late 1800s and early part of the 1900s, private banks made most of the loans people used to buy their homes. Insurance companies also played a huge role in home loan lending.

In the 1970s, home loans began to be issued more by thrifts, or savings and loans (S&Ls) than retail banks. Credit unions also began to play a role in mortgage lending during this time. S&Ls thrived for decades until the late 1980s, when many S&Ls were shut down or otherwise went out of business. Mortgage banks began to fill the void left behind by the S&L collapse.

In this era, most home loans were conventional ones underwritten to Fannie Mae or Freddie Mac guidelines. Very soon thereafter, in the early 1990s, mortgage brokers began their ascent to the mortgage origination mountain, which by the early 2000s commanded nearly two-thirds of residential mortgage loan origination.

As that decade came to an end, the influence of the mortgage broker began to wane, as many major mortgage companies stopped using mortgage brokers to market their mortgage loans for them and instead used their own retail presence to market directly to the public.

At no time did these various institutions simply vanish, rather they increased or decreased their market share. This shifting of market share can be caused by a variety of factors—sometimes by economic forces, sometimes by marketing, or by a combination of the two. You can get your mortgage at a bank down the street. You can go to your credit union. Mortgage bankers offer mortgage loans, as do mortgage brokers. You can even go online to find a lender.

So if there are so many different players in the mortgage business, where is the best place to get a mortgage loan? The answer to that is to first understand how all these different sources for mortgage money operate and who they really are.

CHANGING PRESENCE OF BANKS IN THE MORTGAGE INDUSTRY

Banks are the easiest to spot and perhaps the oldest source of home loans. They're easy to spot, they're on street corners everywhere it seems, and they typically have the word "bank" somewhere on their storefront. Chase Bank. Bank of America. Compass Bank. Bank of New York. Pretty easy, no? But their presence in the mortgage industry has changed dramatically over the past century.

The biggest change regarding banks now and banks just a few short years ago is that there are fewer of them. Some of the biggest banks in the country were shut down by the Fed or acquired by another bank. Initially, in the late 1800s and into the mid-1900s, banks made home loans, but they did so primarily from the deposits in their vaults. Quite frankly, mostly rich people could get loans because they also had the money required for the sizable down payment.

As banks evolved, they drew money from their own credit lines and would decide to sell the loan to someone else to replenish their credit line and make more loans, or they could keep the loan and collect the monthly payments and make their profits from the interest the bank charged. Credit unions and S&Ls operate in much the same fashion; they can issue loans from their own funds or make a loan from a credit account previously set up.

Mortgage banks also make mortgage loans, but they're distinguished from the previous three institutions in that the only thing mortgage banks do is make mortgage loans. They don't offer credit cards or savings accounts; they just make mortgage loans. Mortgage banks are not as easy to identify just from their name. A mortgage banker might be called something like "Reed Mortgage" or "Reed Capital" or some such.

CHANGING ROLE OF MORTGAGE BROKERS

A mortgage broker is different than all other sources for mortgage money. Mortgage brokers don't have credit lines to draw from nor do they have any money in their vaults to make a mortgage loan. A broker is someone who acts as an agent that brings lender and borrower together. Exactly which lenders does the broker use, and how does the broker find them?

Many mortgage companies have two types of operations, retail and wholesale. A retail mortgage operation is the business unit that works directly with the borrower. A wholesale mortgage company is a business that works with mortgage brokers, who then work directly with the borrower.

It's a wholesale business unit because wholesale lenders in fact offer lower-than-market interest rates to mortgage brokers, who then mark up the mortgage loan program to a more competitive "street," or retail, price level. Common markups from wholesale to retail are usually

0.25 percent. If a mortgage broker quotes 6.00 percent to a borrower, the mortgage broker obtained that mortgage at about 5.75 percent.

Wholesale mortgage lenders use mortgage brokers to market their mortgage products to consumers in lieu of retail loan officers. Mortgage brokers have their own overhead, such as offices, employees, insurance and benefits, supplies, telephone lines—the typical business requirements.

Wholesale lenders avoid these overhead charges needed to run a retail operation and recruit mortgage brokers who already have a business in place. Wholesale lenders employ account executives, or sales reps, who make sales calls on mortgage brokers to recruit mortgage brokerage operations and their bevy of loan officers.

Mortgage brokers came onto the scene in a big way in the late 1980s, primarily pioneered by such lending giants as Countrywide and Bank of America. The business plan of a mortgage brokerage operation made for a rapid expansion of mortgage lending, as mortgage companies didn't have to spend the time and capital needed to open up new retail operations or bank branches. Instead, they found independent mortgage brokers to market for them.

Wholesale mortgage lenders could then distribute their mortgage products in a highly efficient manner, using a business entity already in place with a customer base already established.

Mortgage brokers were largely unregulated and certainly unlicensed. The mortgage broker would apply to market the mortgages for a wholesale lender and had to have good credit and a place of business, but mortgage brokers mostly policed themselves without any regulation from state or federal agencies.

Early in the 1990s, however, that began to change. It became apparent that mortgage brokers were marketing products that should have commanded a bit more attention. If stockbrokers or life insurance agents had to be licensed and regulated, then why not monitor companies that were marketing another financial instrument—mortgages?

The advantage of a mortgage broker was primarily focused in two areas: shopping around for the best rate from various wholesale mortgage companies and passing the savings on to the consumer and finding a unique mortgage program not all lenders would offer.

Shopping for the Best Rate Is Not as Simple as Checking Percentages

Each day, both retail and wholesale mortgage lenders set their interest rates for that business day. We'll discuss in detail how mortgage rates are set in the next chapter. As a wholesale mortgage lender issued its mortgage rates, it would distribute them to its mortgage broker network by fax, e-mail, or with special rate quotes designed around the *loan level pricing adjustment* (LLPA) explained in Chapter 2.

A wholesale rate sheet might look something like this:

30-Year Fixed Wholesale Rates

5.00 percent	2 points
5.125 percent	1.5 points
5.25 percent	1 point
5.375 percent	0.5 points
5.50 percent	0 points

The mortgage broker would review these rates, then add its profit to make the loan competitive with retail. A mortgage broker could take these rates, mark them up by 0.25 percent, or simply add its profit in the form of another point. The new broker retail rate sheet might then look like this:

30-Year Fixed Rates

5.00 percent	3 points
5.125 percent	2.5 points
5.25 percent	2 points
5.375 percent	1.5 points
5.50 percent	1 point

Or a broker could add instead an origination fee, or a mortgage broker fee, or really any fee a broker could think up as long as it remained competitive with the marketplace. A broker might add a 1 percent origination fee. An origination fee is expressed as a percentage of the amount being borrowed. On a $200,000 loan, one origination fee would equal $2,000. Much like a point. The brokers' rate sheet would look like this:

30-Year Fixed Rates

5.00 percent	2 points +	1 origination fee
5.125 percent	1.5 points +	1 origination fee
5.25 percent	1 point +	1 origination fee
5.375 percent	0.5 points +	1 origination fee
5.50 percent	0 points +	1 origination fee

Or it could look like this:

5.00 percent	2 points +	1 percent broker fee
5.125 percent	1.5 points +	1 percent broker fee
5.25 percent	1 point +	1 percent broker fee
5.375 percent	0.5 points +	1 percent broker fee
5.50 percent	0 points +	1 percent broker fee

The result to the consumer was the same, regardless if the broker added one point, one origination fee, or 1 percent broker fee. But because the mortgage brokers got wholesale interest rates from multiple wholesale lenders, then the mortgage brokers could compare the various mortgage companies to find the best interest rate for their clients.

A mortgage broker can be signed up with as many wholesale mortgage companies as it sees fit. When shopping around for a mortgage broker, you'll encounter advertising slogans that say something like, "We have over 100 lenders," or, "Let our lenders compete for your business."

In reality, a mortgage broker has no reason to do business with

100 lenders, and I'll just bet that when push comes to shove, there aren't even 100 wholesale lenders in the country. At the very least, a mortgage broker doesn't have 100 lenders at its disposal that they're approved with. But it makes for good marketing. I know, because when I started in this business as a mortgage broker, we touted our 50 lenders we worked with.

The daily routine works like this: As wholesale lenders distributed their mortgage rates to their brokers, the brokers would then scour those rate sheets to find the absolute best lender for that day.

I can recall when I first got into this business as a mortgage broker many years ago. Each morning, I would stand by the fax machine waiting for all of my mortgage lenders to fax their rates to me. I would pore through them, hoping I would find the one lender that would be better than any other lender, but it was to no avail. Mortgage companies essentially have the very same rates, and they're all offered to mortgage brokers.

The fact of the matter is that lenders can't be wildly apart from one another in interest rate because mortgage companies set their rates on the same index, as discussed in the next chapter.

Rate sheets from two different lenders might look like this:

30-Year Fixed Wholesale Rates

Lender A		Lender B	
5.00 percent	2.0 points	5.00 percent	1.875 points
5.125 percent	1.5 points	5.125 percent	1.375 points
5.25 percent	1.0 point	5.25 percent	1.25 points
5.375 percent	0.5 points	5.375 percent	1.00 point
5.50 percent	0 points	5.50 percent	0.5 points

And that's for just one loan program, a conventional 30-year fixed-rate loan. Now add 25-year loans, 20-year, 15-year, and so on. Rate sheets can be four or five pages long!

The Right Mortgage Program Could Come from a Mortgage Broker—or Not

Perhaps the single biggest change in the mortgage brokerage industry is the fact brokers don't have mortgage programs that other banks, credit unions, savings and loans, and mortgage banks don't have. There is no benefit to using a broker.

Historically, besides trying to shop around for the best interest rate for their clients, brokers can also market hard-to-find mortgage programs. For instance, there might be a special loan program designed for condominiums that have yet to be completed, are primarily rental units, or aren't approved by Fannie, Freddie, VA, or FHA as approved condominiums. Such condos are called "nonwarrantable" condos.

When a client wanted to buy a condo that wasn't considered to be warrantable, the broker would contact a few of its "niche" lenders that would offer mortgage programs that could be found nowhere else. The niche lender would use mortgage brokers to advertise its products, and the brokers would then promote those special loan programs to their clients.

Or a client might have damaged credit and need a loan program that catered to those with bad credit. Or maybe a client had hard-to-prove income. Whatever the issue, if a borrower couldn't get a conventional or government loan, it could always turn to a mortgage broker who could find the special loan program.

No longer. Mortgage loans in the market today are either government-backed or conventional loans underwritten to Fannie or Freddie standards. Mortgage brokers no longer have mortgage programs that other lenders don't have. I can recall in 2005 and 2006 that there was a huge influx of "alternative documentation" loan programs. These were the loans that were acceptable for nonwarrantable condos as previously described or that met other unique borrower requirements. My company only had government and conventional loan programs and simply couldn't compete against brokers who offered such products. Yet that is no longer the case; mortgage brokers have the very same mortgage programs that banks do.

From your perspective, it doesn't matter if you use a bank, mortgage bank, or a broker. A mortgage broker doesn't approve the loan. The broker takes the loan application from the borrowers, pulls a credit report, and begins to document the file. The broker then submits the file electronically to the wholesale lender's AUS for an approval, then proceeds to submit the loan application and supporting documentation in accordance with the loan approval issued by the lender.

Bankers do the same thing, but instead of sending the loan to another company to complete the process, banks keep the loan internally and close the loan themselves.

From a consumer's standpoint, there really is little difference in the result of going to a broker versus a banker; the loan is still approved in much the same fashion. So the mechanics matter little with regard to the method of providing a mortgage to a consumer as long as the loan gets to the consumer in a competitive fashion.

I started my career in the mortgage industry some 20 years ago as a mortgage broker in San Diego. That's how I learned the business. I would take the application, qualify the buyers, review the credit, then attempt to find the best deal possible for my clients.

When I found the best deal, I would send the loan via overnight delivery to the wholesale lender and wait for its approval to be issued. Typically, the wholesale lender would ask for some additional documentation, which I would provide, and then order closing papers that would be delivered to the escrow agent who would handle the closing.

When I moved to Texas in 1995, I began working with a mortgage banker. This company, Partners Mortgage Services, was a small, independent mortgage banker that had its own credit line with a local bank. Partners would document the file, approve the loan, print the closing papers, and deliver them to the settlement agent.

Partners was not a loan servicer; it didn't make money on collecting monthly interest payments but instead sold the loan to other mortgage bankers, who would buy closed loans from other mortgage banks. Most every major national or regional lender had a division designed to buy mortgage loans from smaller mortgage bankers like Partners. Bank of America, Chase, Countrywide—all had departments that catered to mortgage bankers like Partners. This would appear to be exactly how mortgage brokers operate—find clients, then match them up with a lender. On the surface, it might appear that the function between a broker and a banker were the same, but there are some significant differences.

Shh: Small Mortgage Bankers Can Get Better Rates Than Brokers (and They Have More Control Over the Loan)

Primarily, the difference is that the mortgage banker provides the underwriting (approving) of the loan, prepares the loan documents, and delivers them to the settlement agent and prepares and packages the loan to sell to the mortgage bank agreeing to buy the loan. These activities represent a significant amount of overhead the buying mortgage bank doesn't have to provide.

The selling bank warrants the fact that the loan meets government or conventional guidelines and the loan is then eligible for sale on the secondary market. In exchange for not only originating the loan from the borrower, underwriting, documenting, and delivering a closed loan, the originating bank would get better mortgage rates than a mortgage broker could get.

This is a little-known facet of the mortgage industry that smaller mortgage bankers can actually get better pricing than brokers can—

plus, they have more control over the loan. How much better? Typically, it's imperceptible, but sometimes banks can get 0.25 to 0.5 point better than brokers can get. Besides price—and, in my opinion, more importantly—bankers have control over the loan that mortgage brokers just don't have. Once the broker sends the loan to a wholesale lender, the wholesale lender takes control of the loan, issues loan papers, and decides what additional documentation will be required: This, of course, assumes that the loan is in fact an approvable mortgage loan.

Mortgage bankers, by contrast, use all their employees in the loan process, not just the loan officer. When there is a problem with a brokered loan, the loan officer is ultimately contacted by the account executive and says, "Hey Dave, we're going to have to decline this loan. The husband's credit score is too low," or some such.

The loan officer then tries to figure out how to get the loan approved and then has to resubmit the mortgage loan all over again. In this example, the loan officer took the husband off of the loan and qualified them with just the wife's income. The loan is resubmitted under the new arrangement, and the process starts all over again.

Mortgage banks can decline the loan, but instead of the loan decision being made through an array of people, the underwriter can call the loan officer, and say, "Dave, we can't do this loan with the husband on the loan. Do you want to take him off and just qualify using the wife's income?"

"Sure." And the loan continues to move forward. I learned this advantage first hand when one of my first loans as a mortgage banker had a problem just a day before the closing; I noticed the loan papers had the wrong interest rate—it was higher by an eighth of a percent. I was mortified. Here was one of my first loans in Texas, and it was going south. I would never get another referral from the Realtor involved in the deal again!

Because I was used to the fact that brokered loans would have to sometimes start all the way back at square one, I was facing the prospect that my loan papers wouldn't make it to closing on time. This was something that I was used to expecting would add days to the loan process.

I told my boss what happened, and he told me to call the underwriter and explain what happened.

"The rate says 8.125 percent but should be 8.00 percent. What do I do?"

"Nothing," she said. "I'll make the change."

She did make the change in a matter of minutes. My loan papers were corrected, and I closed my first loan as a banker. Bankers and brokers will always be competitive on price, but bankers have a superior advantage over brokers in controlling the loan process.

Finally, mortgage brokers can no longer order appraisals. This also widens the control gap. When a borrower applies for a mortgage from either a broker or banker, the loan officer will eventually order an appraisal. This doesn't sound like that big of a deal, but it is.

The state of New York took a lender to court regarding some loan shenanigans. The lender was nationally known, and the suit was aimed at the wholesale division. Among other things, the state of New York alleged corruption between a loan officer and the appraiser. Loan officers were pressuring appraisers to come in at a required value. If the appraiser said he didn't think the value would be what was needed, the loan officer would threaten to take his business elsewhere.

HOME VALUATION CODE OF CONDUCT

As previously discussed, appraisals are an integral part of the loan approval process. Lenders use appraisals not just to determine the value of the property in question but also to set the maximum loan amount a lender can lend. Yet appraisals can be manipulated. An appraisal will have a minimum of three closed sales within a local area but the underwriter won't have additional data at their disposal that might dispute the appraisal.

If a loan officer, who might be paid 100 percent on commission, had a refinance loan of, say, $300,000, yet the values of local sales showed the value to be only $295,000, there would be no loan issued. That means no commission check. For a $300,000 conventional refinance, typically there needs to be a minimum value of $333,000.

So what if there were other sales, perhaps a bit further out than the comps closer to the subject? What if the appraiser used bad comps to support a $333,000 value and not the comps listed on the very same street as the subject property?

If the appraiser used the bad comps, the underwriter might not ever know. The underwriter may not have closed sale data on the neighborhood where the subject property is located. As long as the bad comps were within 12 months old and followed typical appraisal guidelines, then the loan could go ahead and be approved.

Now the loan officer closes the mortgage, makes a commission, and the appraiser makes money from the appraisal. The next time the loan officer needs an appraisal, he'll call up his appraiser buddy and go through the whole routine all over again.

The loan officer and appraiser have a special relationship, and like other business relationships, if not held in moral check can be abused. Think of someone selling stock based on insider information. The stockholder found out from her friend at corporate that the quarterly earnings report was going to be dismal, so the stockholder sold all her shares before the bad news was released, profiting from the insider dealings. This is insider trading, and it is illegal.

Loan officers and appraisers have been working hand in hand for decades with no problems. But just like any other business, there are bad guys who manipulate the system.

When it was discovered that appraisals in some instances were being manipulated by loan officers, appraisers, and even real estate agents, the end result was, partially, the Home Valuation Code of Conduct, or HVCC.

The HVCC, which took effect in 2009, addresses several lender-appraiser issues but mainly attempts to halt a loan officer from coercing an appraiser into coming in with a particular value.

The HVCC identifies as illegal actions coercion, inducement, extortion, instruction, collusion, intimidation, compensation, and bribery. All such actions to get to a particular value would violate the HVCC.

A loan officer might sit at her desk and, seeing that she might have some value issues with a potential deal (read: commission check), she could start making phone calls to different appraisers and saying things like this:

"If you don't make value, then I'll never use you again."

"If you can make value, then I'll throw in another $500."

"Make sure the value comes in at $300,000."

"If this appraisal doesn't come in at what we need, I'll blackball you from our database."

The HVCC addresses all these statements and attempts to eliminate them. The truth is that bad people will be bad people regardless of what the law says, so the HVCC tries to eliminate the temptation altogether by removing the mortgage broker from ordering the appraisal directly from the appraiser altogether.

Now mortgage brokers can't coerce, induce, extort, instruct, collude, intimidate, compensate, or bribe an appraiser. This itself is monitored by the wholesale lender, who makes certain the appraisal meets HVCC standards.

But mortgage banks aren't off the hook entirely, either. Though a mortgage banker or bank isn't prohibited from ordering an appraisal directly, the HVCC does prohibit anyone that works for the mortgage bank that would profit directly from the loan closing.

This was initially meant to encompass loan officers or production supervisors who might get a commission check when the deal closed, cutting off the temptation of trying to influence a value in order to make money.

Unfortunately, the wording of the code is unclear. Does a loan processor profit when a loan closes? Can she order the appraisal? After all, she's not getting paid solely on whether the deal closes. She gets her regular paycheck, regardless of any particular deal closing or not closing. But does she not also profit if a loan closes? In fact, doesn't the entire company profit when the processor does what the business is designed to do: close loans? Of course. While it's clear a loan officer of a mortgage bank can't order an appraisal directly from the appraiser, the company can, as long as no one who orders the appraisal profits directly from the closing of the loan.

Appraisals Are Now More Money

Mortgage banks addressed the HVCC guidelines in two ways: a rotating wheel and an appraisal management firm.

A rotating wheel is nothing more than ordering an appraisal simply based on "whose turn is it next?" without regards to any particular value or appraiser. If a lender has 10 appraisers in its database then appraisals will be ordered consecutively, with each appraiser waiting in line.

The next approach is to have an appraisal management company order the appraisals. These firms are independent third parties who manage the appraisal process by ordering the appraisals on behalf of the loan officer or lender, receive them, and then forward them to the lender.

On the surface, the HVCC appears to eliminate the coercion and extortion that can exist between a loan officer and an appraiser. But as with many government-induced programs, it has its drawbacks. It raised the cost of appraisals. Appraisal management companies find appraisers to join their network. Appraisal management companies then solicit lenders to use their services. How do appraisal management companies get paid? Primarily from reducing the appraisers fees. If an appraiser normally charges $400 for an appraisal, by signing on with an appraisal management company the appraiser may have to agree to charge less, say $200. The appraisal management company would then keep the difference.

Okay, so what? If the cost to the consumer doesn't change, who cares who gets the money? Appraisers do, and if they make half of what they used to make, what would they ultimately do? Charge more for the appraisal itself, or quit the industry?

The Relationship with Appraisers Has Changed

Since the loan officer can't communicate directly with the appraiser, what would happen if the consumer chose to go to a different lender? If you change lenders you might have to pay for an appraisal twice. Historically, the loan officer would order a "retype," which would remove the old lenders name and put the new name in its place.

That would work if the new lender was a member of the appraisal management company. The lender would order a retype, but it's likely that a whole new appraisal would have to be ordered if the appraiser is not a member of the appraisal management company. That means the consumer pays $800 for appraisals, not $400.

Before the HVCC, a loan officer would call the appraiser and ask for an approximate value for a refinance. Now, however, the loan officer can't do that. That makes it important to talk to your loan officer when filling out your initial loan application.

There is a section on page 1 of the application that asks for the "estimated value." Most often, this field is left blank and only completed after the loan is approved. Instead, consult with your loan officer to find out what the value might come in at and shoot for the high side. Enter that amount in the field when completing the application. This way, the value will be communicated to the appraisal management company, who is able to communicate the value to the appraiser.

Although eliminating a working relationship between a loan officer and an appraiser sounds like a good idea, in fact it throws the baby out with the bath water. The appraiser/loan officer relationship was important to me, and ultimately important to the consumer.

If there were an issue with a possible valuation problem, I could call up the appraiser I've used for the past 10 years and say, "Hey, here's a potential problem. Can you look up 123 Main Street and see if we might get a value of $200,000 or so?"

The appraiser would run some numbers and check recent sales and call me back with a "Yes, it looks like that value will come in," or, "Not sure until we look at the property," or, "No way." With that information, I could talk to the consumer and say yes, maybe, or no. The consumer would then decide whether to move forward and spend money for a new appraisal. With the HVCC, that option has vanished.

NATIONAL REGISTRY FOR LICENSED MORTGAGE LOAN OFFICERS

New regulations aren't just limited to appraisals and loan programs; they also now apply to loan officers, specifically as it applies to licensing. Recall that wholesale mortgage lenders find mortgage brokers to market their products, but how does the wholesale lender know where to find these brokers in the first place? They first start with the governing board in the broker's state that regulates and licenses mortgage brokers.

In the past, mortgage brokers were regulated and licensed by their individual state. Oklahoma has different licensing laws than Texas. In California, when I first became a mortgage broker, I was licensed and monitored by the California Department of Real Estate.

Mortgage bankers and employees of banks are typically regulated separately than brokers. When I was with a major bank, as loan officers we were not individually licensed. Banks come under some severe scrutiny as it is, with their own host of compliance and regulatory issues they must face. Brokers have complained for years that mortgage bankers and banks don't fall under the same scrutiny as mortgage brokers do. And they're right; they come under *more* regulation.

Banks are regulated by the Fed, the FDIC, the Office of Currency Comptroller, the Department of Housing and Urban Development, and FHA. In the case of mortgage banks, they too must meet minimum standards both in terms of net worth, loan quality, and liquidity. It's no easy task to obtain a credit line and be approved by HUD, Fannie, or Freddie to underwrite and sell mortgage loans.

Although brokers have complained that they're being licensed more than mortgage bankers, that fact is just the opposite. Mortgage brokers may have had more individual loan officer licenses simply because there were more of them, and in certain states individual mortgage bankers didn't have to license their individual loan officers as long as the mortgage bank was qualified to sell loans to Fannie, Freddie, or FHA.

Still, mortgage banks are regulated in most every state. Often not in the same fashion as mortgage brokers, but regulated nonetheless. In California, for instance, mortgage bankers are regulated by the State Department of Corporations, while brokers are regulated by the Department of Real Estate.

Now, however, every single loan officer not employed by a bank is licensed and registered with the federal government. Broker or banker, both must not only be licensed in accordance with their state laws but also registered and assigned a unique identifier that stays with that loan officer for the remainder of his career regardless of where he ends up working.

This national registry performs a background check on each individual loan officer and keeps tabs on the loan officers, as long as they're working in the mortgage field. This is probably long overdue, in my opinion. While I'm not a big fan of government regulations, the fact remained that the entry level for being a loan officer was next to nothing. Employees of pawn shops and so-called payday lenders endured more scrutiny. Frankly, due to the potential for fraud, anyone with an ounce of intentions to cheat as a loan officer picked the wrong industry. Imagine being a crook, taking a loan application, and then having at your disposal the names, social security numbers, and bank account information of all your "clients." Think there might be a bit of temptation there? Apparently, there was plenty of it in the 2000s, and we're still paying the price today.

NEW LICENSING RULES

Loan officers are at least registered with a single government entity, but that doesn't really level the license playing field. Depository institutions, or institutions that take consumers' deposits in the form of savings or checking accounts, are not required to have their individual loan officers licensed. Again, simply being a bank places more regulations than any individual loan officer could imagine.

Mortgage banks do have to be registered, as do their loan officers in a similar fashion as brokers do with one major exception: yield spread premiums.

There Are New Disclosure Requirements for Yield Spread Premiums

Yield spread premiums, or YSPs, is the latest moniker given to an amount of income a broker receives from the wholesale lender. Yes, that's right. A wholesale lender can pay a mortgage broker on your mortgage loan. Is that a form of bribery? It might appear that way, but in reality it's not, and here's how YSPs come into play.

Recall that the lower the rate, the more points you'd pay? Here's the chart we reviewed earlier:

30-Year Fixed Rates

5.00 percent	3.0 points
5.125 percent	2.5 points
5.25 percent	2.0 points
5.375 percent	1.5 points
5.50 percent	1.0 point

Now add some rates with a YSP.

5.625 percent	0.5 points
5.75 percent	0 points
5.875 percent	− 0.50 points
6.00 percent	− 1.00 points

Using this example, if you wanted a 5.00 percent rate, you'd have to pay three points. Or pay one point to get the higher 5.50 percent rate. By increasing the rate even higher, soon the "points" become negative. "Negative" points mean the rate is so much higher than for ones with points that there are points left over—to the loan officer or to the consumer in the form of yield spread premium.

For instance, this chart would have a 6.00 percent rate at −1.00 points. On a $200,000 loan, that would mean there is $2,000 available from the lender in exchange for a higher interest rate. Lenders quite frankly don't care if someone pays points or not. A lender will issue a lower rate for more points and charge no points for a higher rate. The end result is typically the same for the lender. But not for the mortgage broker, who has to disclose the additional income that a lender is offering. This is called the "disclosure" rule and was implemented early on in my career as a mortgage broker in California.

A mortgage broker is supposed to declare any and all compensation in mortgage transaction. Brokers thought this was unfair, but in reality, every other business entity also has to disclose what they're making. The real estate agents disclose their commissions, appraisers disclose how much their appraisals cost, and title insurance shows what the charges are.

Changes in RESPA Help Consumers

This is all required due to the Real Estate Settlement Procedures Act, or RESPA. All financial transactions must be disclosed to the borrowers. RESPA was designed to thwart back-door referral fees from one party to the next. Say a real estate agent referred the name of an insurance agent to provide a policy. Although it's not illegal to refer an insurance agent, it's illegal to refer an insurance agent and get a referral fee for doing so.

RESPA forced all parties to disclose who charged what and who paid for it. That's when the YSP began to come into play.

Back in the late 1980s and early 1990s, disclosure of a YSP wasn't a requirement. Back then, it wasn't called a YSP but a "rebate." As interest rate choices to the consumer rose, rebates would be provided to the broker, who would then pass along that rebate to the consumer or keep the rebate themselves as additional profit on the loan. It wasn't a requirement to disclose to the borrower that there was a rebate involved.

But as there are so many rate and point combinations, it soon became evident that to comply with RESPA any rebate had to be disclosed to the borrower—after all, it was income paid by one party to another in the course of a real estate transaction.

In 1991, rebates were for the first time required to be disclosed by mortgage brokers to their clients. Personally, I never had an issue with disclosing when I was a broker. I always touted our "no point, no fee" mortgage loan program and actually showed my wholesale lenders rate sheet that I received to the client, which explained the process.

"In exchange for a slightly higher rate, we can cover your closing costs for you while at the same time having the lender pay our fee," was a typical presentation.

Disclosing rebates has been a sore spot for mortgage brokers for years, claiming that it's unfair to disclose all their income, including YSPs, when mortgage bankers aren't required to disclose YSP.

A mortgage broker might have a YSP that is disclosed to the borrower when a mortgage banker, offering the very same rate, might have some similar amount built into the loan as well but the borrowers are not told about it—unless they ask.

The brokers have a good point. It doesn't seem fair. All parties are supposed to disclose who is making how much off of the real estate transaction. But for a mortgage banker, the final profit may not be known on a particular loan for several days after the loan has closed. Or longer. Yes, the rate might be 6.00 percent at the closing table, but if the lender decides to keep that loan and not sell it, the profit to the banker would be much more than just the 6.00 percent rate at the closing table. It would be thousands upon thousands of dollars collected in long-term interest.

If the mortgage bank does in fact decide to sell the loan, at what rate and at what fee does the banker sell it for? Loans can be sold at a profit or at a potential loss, depending on market conditions. For instance, a mortgage bank has several loans it closed at 6.00 percent, and the mortgage bank wants to sell them to raise money. But the rates had moved down since the original close dates to 5.00 percent. Instead of those loans being worth 6.00 percent, they sell them closer to market conditions and, in effect, take a loss on those loans.

That's why disclosing by direct lenders of all the profit on a mortgage loan at closing can't be determined. Any YSP by a banker may not be the profit on the loan; there are too many other potential costs involved to make that determination. Brokers make their money at the settlement table and move on. Bankers hold onto that asset and value it differently as markets change.

Brokers had in the past disclosed YSP as a "range" of potential rebate, and this disclosure comes in the form of the *good faith estimate*, or GFE, that must be provided to the borrowers at the initial meeting between the loan officer and the borrowers or within three days if the application was received via mail, fax, or online. The GFE highlights all the potential charges a borrower might incur while obtaining a mortgage.

The broker would disclose to the borrower something like, "Your rate, if you locked in today, would be 6.00 percent, I would charge a 1 percent origination fee, and there might be some yield spread premium. This yield spread premium is paid directly to me by the lender and could be anywhere from 0 to 3 percent of the loan amount." On a $200,000 loan, that range could be anywhere from zero to $6,000. That's hardly an accurate disclosure, but the brokers used that method for years.

Until now. Brokers must disclose to the borrower any YSP not to exceed a certain amount of money. If the broker initially disclosed to the borrower that the broker would be making 1 percent in YSP on a $200,000 loan, or $2,000, and the actually YSP came in at 1.25 percent in YSP, then the broker would either have to give the additional 0.25 percent to the borrower in the form of a credit or disclose once again to the borrower the higher YSP.

Why don't brokers know how much YSP they will be getting at the initial application? Because interest rates change over time, and unless the loan is "locked in," that rate as well as the YSP will float along with the market. We'll discuss rates and locks in detail in Chapter 6.

If the YSP is higher upon locking than originally disclosed, the wholesale lender will not release the loan until the new disclosure forms are signed.

Direct Lenders Have the Upper Hand

So which is better, a broker or a banker? For definition purposes, a banker means a retail bank, savings and loan, credit union, or mort-

gage bank—anyone who approves and provides the funds for a mortgage.

Since interest rates can't be that much different from one lender
to the next, be it comparing a broker to a banker, it may not matter
all that much where the mortgage loan comes from. Personally, I
think it's best to go with a mortgage banker as long as the rates are
as competitive as can be found from a mortgage broker. Mortgage
brokers certainly have access to multiple wholesale lenders, and on
any given day one or two lenders might be 0.25 of a point better than
the rest of the market.

Note that this is a *quarter of a point*, not 0.25 percent in interest
rate. If you're being quoted 6.00 percent at 1.00 point and the broker
can get 0.25 in YSP, it's not very likely you'll get that 0.25 point for
you to apply to your closing costs. It's possible, just not likely. Mortgage brokers will shop around to different lenders—not necessarily
to get you a better rate but a competitive one, while finding a little bit
extra for themselves.

If you found a mortgage broker who could find a 5.75 percent
rate while everyone else was at 6.00 percent for the same amount of
money, then certainly use the mortgage broker. But unless the broker
is doing the loan for free, you can't expect that much disparity in rate.

What if you do get a quote at 6.00 percent for 1.00 point and the
broker discloses to you that there's another 0.50 point available in
the form of YSP? Why not ask for it? That's right, tell the broker that
you see there's an additional 0.50 point from the lender and can she
apply that 0.50 point toward your closing costs.

YSPs Are Negotiable

Consumers aren't typically aware that the YSP is negotiable and figure that it's simply something the wholesale lender is paying the
broker for sending a loan to them. It's not; the YSP is nothing more
than a by-product of the interest rate selected by the consumer or the
broker. So go ahead and ask for it. It doesn't hurt to do so, and you'll
probably get some of it.

ADVANTAGES OF MORTGAGE BANKERS

If brokers can't be hands down the best all the time, then I suggest using a banker due to the control of the loan the banker has. But not just any old banker. National banks with a presence seemingly everywhere, or older, established institutions have an inherent advantage when it comes to their interest rates; they don't have to be the lowest in order to get a consumer's business.

The big lenders have a loyal following and can offer more than just a mortgage by issuing credit cards or keeping someone's checking or savings account. That loyalty factor will result in slightly higher rates than what can be found through a mortgage broker or smaller mortgage bank.

In fact, the best choice might be a pure-play mortgage bank. These business types offer nothing but mortgages and have to be competitive in the marketplace to compete with brokers. In addition to always being competitive, the mortgage bank has complete control of the loan file from start to finish.

Mortgage banks view loan files a bit differently than a mortgage broker might. Mortgage bankers have a sense of ownership on the loan file that brokers may not have. This is different than committing to excellent customer service or keeping in contact with old clients.

Mortgage bankers originate, process, underwrite, fund, and sell or service your loan. If the loan is sold and for some reason it goes bad, the loan gets sent back to the original lender. Mortgage bankers have to be certain their loan is a good loan, or else they'll have a loan on their hands they don't want or can't afford.

Mortgage bankers work as a team. If someone in the underwriting department has a question on a loan application, the underwriter will simply call or e-mail the loan processor or loan officer. "Are the borrowers married? They have different last names." Or, "Who is the person giving the financial gift to the buyers? What relation are they?"

It may sound simplistic, but lenders who view loans as their own "baby" and watch it grow up can move loans more efficiently than a broker can. Ownership goes far beyond the loan closing. A mortgage broker originates the loan, documents it, and then submits it to the wholesale lender. The wholesale lender completes the loan process and pays the broker at the closing table. The broker moves on to the next loan.

Additionally, some of the largest banks in the country that used the mortgage broker channel have closed their wholesale operations altogether and no longer use brokers. Many lenders who used brokers, sometimes exclusively, are no longer in business, and there are fewer mortgage brokers today than there were just a few short years ago.

It's hard sometimes to determine if you're talking to a broker or a banker simply based on the name. You might find companies that have "mortgage bankers" in their name so that would be a start, but you may have to do a little research. One way to tell is to visit their websites and review the "About Us" section. Or at the bottom of the main page, it should say something to the effect of "Licensed as a Mortgage Broker" or "Licensed as a Mortgage Banker."

Disclaimer: My primary experience has been a pure play mortgage bank and that's what I do now, so maybe I'm biased. But I have worked with a mortgage brokerage operation, a pure-play mortgage bank, and at the time the nineteenth largest retail bank in the country in my 20 years in the business. I've worked all three options.

You won't find a mortgage banker with the name of something like "ABC Mortgage Bank We Don't Do Anything Else But Mortgages," but instead something that sounds like any other mortgage company: "XYZ Capital" or "Super Mortgage."

Does all that mean you should only contact mortgage bankers to find the best loan officer? Of course not. There are some very good loan officers that work at mortgage brokerage firms. There are some very good loan officers that work in retail banks and credit unions and savings and loan companies. It's just that the business model of a mortgage banker is more in tune with consumers' requirements in light of today's market.

When there was a plethora of subprime loans, alternative loans, and "no document" loans, then brokers had a distinct advantage over their peers. Now that almost everyone has the same loan choices and rates are competitive, the utility of a broker has weakened.

FINDING A GOOD LOAN OFFICER

How do you identify a good loan officer? The best loan officers have been around for a while. They've gained experience in the lending industry. This isn't uncommon for any business—those who have been in the business longer than others are either lucky or very good at what they do. But in the lending business there's an additional reason why years in the business is critical: automated underwriting.

AUS applications introduced in the late 1990s marked a brand new way of approving loans. It streamlined the process, while at the same time cutting out certain efficiencies in the mortgage industry. It made my life and my loan processors' lives a whole lot easier (see Chapter 4 for more details).

With an AUS, a loan officer simply "plugs in" the loan application data, hits the "send" button and within a few seconds the loan approval is issued along with a list of required information to close the loan.

AUS applications really made it big in the early 2000s, right about the same time as rates hit then-record lows and so many people were refinancing their home loan. Over the next few years, the nation enjoyed a substantial housing boom with home sales all across the country setting new records. With this new influx of both purchase and refinance business, lots of people quit what they were doing and went to work as loan officers. There wasn't really a whole lot to learn, just open the door and let some new business walk in. The new loan officer didn't need to know how loans were approved just how to enter the loan information into the AUS and wait for the approval.

Loan guidelines became more and more relaxed, which resulted in even more loans. New loan officers thought themselves fairly smart when they were "approving" all those new loans. Soon, of course, the housing bubble burst, and lots of loan officers went out of business and went back to what they were doing before.

But if loan officers never understand how loans are approved in the first place by reviewing credit histories, calculating debt ratios, and putting people in the correct loan program, then they won't know what to do when a loan gets turned down.

"Sorry," the loan officer says. "But your loan has been turned down."

"Why?" you say.

"Not sure exactly. This is all I can do."

Automated underwriting systems were designed to streamline the process, not make up for lack of mortgage skills. Loan officers who have been around pre-1997, before the AUS applications came into full force, know how to manually approve a loan. They know how much someone can afford before the loan is submitted to the AUS. They know how to fit monthly payments in order to meet debt ratio requirements. They know the nuances of the various loan programs and which ones will work and which ones will not.

I recall a client who worked in the marketing department for the corporate offices of one of the world's largest real estate companies. She had been shopping for her first home, and obviously working for a large real estate organization allowed her to choose almost any real estate agent she wanted to. She had read one of my books and decided to give me a call.

"David, I'm having trouble getting qualified. I found a house and made an offer, but I'm getting declined and my mortgage broker says I have to wait to save up some more money," she said. In fact, the mortgage broker she was working with was referred to her by her own real estate agent. She told me her situation, and after a few minutes, I said, "Stop right there. You're on the wrong loan program. I can fix this."

Sure enough, she had beaten her head against the wall while her mortgage broker was submitting her loan to this lender and that lender trying to get an approval, but she kept getting turned down time after time—for the very same reason. The broker kept thinking that maybe if she submitted the loan enough times, then certainly some lender would finally approve her.

She had great credit, good income, and a down payment. So what was the problem?

She was putting 10 percent down, and her down payment money was coming from a gift from her father. The mortgage broker was submitting her to different wholesale lenders on a conventional Fannie loan.

The problem was that conventional lenders require 5 percent down from the borrowers' very own funds if the gift represented less than 20 percent of the sales price of the home. The gift was for 10 percent. She didn't have 5 percent of her own money saved up, and that's why she kept getting declined. She applied on my website, I downloaded the application and ran her loan through FHA's automated underwriting system. Voila! Approval!

FHA only requires a borrower to have $500 in a transaction when there is a gift involved. But the mortgage broker wasn't familiar with FHA loans or apparently intelligent enough to know that submitting the same file over and over again under the same guidelines will have the very same result.

This client had been trying to close on her house for nearly two months and had thought she was going to lose the house. In fact, had she not called me or another experienced loan officer she might still be waiting.

If you can find a loan officer that has been in the business since before 1997, you can bet two things:

1. The loan officer is good enough to be in the business for this long to weather the ups and downs in the industry.
2. The loan officer knows the inner workings of loan programs and legitimate ways to get deals closed when others can't.

It's possible that you don't know where to start to find the best loan officer.

□ □ □ □ □ □

There are some tips to help you find a good loan officer, but first, I'll tell you where not to look: the Internet.

□ □ □ □ □ □

There are websites such as Bankrate.com that post interest rates from various lenders. Bankrate.com has plenty of market commentary and actually some very good articles about lending in general and some specific articles on mortgage loans. It also lets lenders pay to advertise on its site. Bankrate.com has a grid with different lenders (most likely none you've ever heard of) showing their company information, their rates, and the different loan programs they might offer.

It's a real shell game, because it's hard to determine who actually has the best rate. In fact, you'll see some phenomenally good rates—some seen nowhere else! In truth, this can be nothing more than a bait-and-switch tactic. Remember, lenders set their rates on the very same index every day, and one lender can't be remarkably lower than anyone else. It just can't happen.

Even if you did decide to use one of those lenders, you're likely to get hooked up with a 1–800 number and a customer service person who lives nowhere near where you do. Mortgage loans can be too complicated to leave to a customer service person. You need someone local who has established themselves in the lending industry.

If you don't have a favorite loan officer you like to use or you can't stand the last one you had, then I suggest finding some good real estate agents in your area and ask them for referrals. Good mortgage loan officers build their businesses around top agents, and they keep those top agents happy by providing their clients with competitive rates and solid customer service.

Okay, so maybe not all of the loan officers out there have gray hair. Maybe they've only been in the business for a few years. I'll grant that everyone has to start in any business at some point, and someone is always a rookie at least once. But this is your mortgage, and you'll be paying on it long after the loan officer shakes your hand thanking you for your business. You want all the competitive edge you can get.

SUMMARY

- ➤ Banks, savings and loans, credit unions, mortgage bankers, and mortgage brokers are all sources for mortgage money.
- ➤ Only mortgage brokers do not lend their own money but find it on behalf of the borrower.
- ➤ Mortgage brokers became increasingly regulated, along with a new national registration process for all loan officers.
- ➤ Mortgage brokers have the ability to compare rates from different wholesale lenders, but since rates are so competitive, the difference is often imperceptible.
- ➤ Shopping around for the "niche" loan program is no longer a benefit, as all lenders now offer the same programs since subprime and alternative lenders went away.
- ➤ The Home Valuation Code of Conduct dramatically changed the way appraisals are ordered and managed.

> Additional appraisal requirements add to the cost of an appraisal.
> "Pure play" mortgage bankers offer competitive rates, plus control of the loan process.
> The best loan officers have been in business prior to the introduction of automated underwriting systems.

Loan Programs:
Which Is Right for You?

RECENT CHANGES in the mortgage industry are many. Many loan programs are disappearing, which makes it even more critical to determine the right mortgage program at the outset. At one point in the mid-2000s, the subprime and alternative loans made up about 40 percent of all the mortgages made.

Suddenly, loan programs began popping up from seemingly out of nowhere, sometimes appearing to accommodate a potential market that was unable to qualify for a home loan. Someone with bad credit? No problem, here's a new loan for you. No down payment? No problem.

 About 40 percent of all mortgage programs have gone away.

As those loans finally went away, the stalwarts remain. Those stalwarts are conventional loans from Fannie and Freddie and government-backed loans (VA, FHA, and USDA).

Government loans still play a key role for those who qualify, and there are even a few portfolio lenders who are still in the mortgage game catering to specific clients. Portfolio lenders are companies that make their own mortgage loans with no intention of selling them in the secondary market or to other lenders. They instead keep them in their own "portfolio."

When deciding which loan program is right for you, it is first best to analyze your current financial situation based on credit, income, amount you want to borrow, and the amount you have available for down payment.

If you have good credit, your debt ratios are in line with typical guidelines, and you have 20 percent or more available as a down payment plus closing costs then you have your choice of loan programs. You can go conventional or you can go government.

Government loans will require a mortgage insurance premium in the case of FHA loans regardless of the amount down. This will add an additional monthly payment should you select an FHA loan. VA loans also have their funding fee, usually 2.15 percent of the loan amount. Although you can roll the funding fee into your loan, there is no need to take a VA loan if you have down payment money, regardless if you're a qualifying veteran.

If the down payment is not a problem for you and you have 20 percent or more down, then you should choose a conventional mortgage. Conventional loans underwritten to Fannie Mae and Freddie Mac guidelines are the most common mortgage type there is and they are offered by both direct mortgage lenders and mortgage brokers.

When there is a lot of something and a lot of businesses are trying to sell it, it follows that the price of that product would be low due to the amount of competition there is in the market.

CONVENTIONAL LOANS

If you have 20 percent for a down payment, go conventional. The same goes for conventional mortgages. You'll find the lowest rates at the lowest cost when you go conventional. There really is no reason to look any further or listen to sales pitches from loan officers trying to talk you into other loan programs.

Having 20 percent down also negates the requirement for mortgage insurance. Recall that any first mortgage with less than that amount down will require a mortgage insurance policy to be in place. Having 20 percent down also means you're not required to escrow your tax and insurance payments. Called "impounds" in various parts of the country, escrow accounts are set up to collect one-twelfth of your annual homeowners insurance and property tax bills. As your property taxes become due, your lender will pay your property tax bill on your behalf from the escrow account you established. The same goes for your homeowners insurance policy. As the insurance policy comes up for renewal, there are funds in your escrow account that have accumulated to be used to automatically renew your insurance policy.

Conventional vs. FHA Loans

With less than 20 percent down, you as a consumer don't have a choice—escrow or impound accounts will be required. If you have less than 20 percent down, say 10 or 15 percent down, conventional loans are less of a hands-down decision, but it does take some math to decide your best route.

First, determine the loan amount won't exceed the FHA limits for your area. You do this by visiting HUD's website at https://entp .hud.gov/idapp/html/hicostlook.cfm. If your loan amount will be above the limits shown on the site, then you'll need to stay in the conventional loan market. If your loan amount will be at or below the limits shown, then proceed to compare the FHA and conventional offerings with both 10 and 15 percent down. Let's do this with a $200,000 sales price and a market rate of 5.50 percent on a 30-year loan.

	Conventional	FHA
Loan amount	$180,000	$180,000
MIP (FHA)		$ 3,150
Final loan amount	$180,000	$183,150
Payment	$1,022	$1,039
MI payment	93	76
Total with MI	$1,115	$1,115

Did you see what happened? We'll explore FHA loans in more detail later on in this chapter, but the total monthly payments for a conventional and FHA are the same. Notice a couple of things, though.

FHA requires an upfront MIP at 1.75 percent of the loan amount, or $3,150 in this example, to be paid at closing. This is an FHA cost that you can include with your loan amount, and since it is relatively substantial, most borrowers do in fact roll it into the loan, increasing the amount borrowed, rather than paying for it out of pocket.

While the monthly payments are similar for both FHA and conventional, the increased loan amount will increase the amount of interest paid over the life of the loan when choosing an FHA loan. In addition, the monthly MIP payment remains during the life of the loan as well.

With conventional mortgage insurance, the mortgage insurance payment can go away at some point when the loan amount falls below 80 percent of the current value of the home. For instance, the home was purchased for $200,000 but one year later it appraises at $225,000. Since the $180,000 loan balance is exactly 80 percent of the value, the homeowner can contact his mortgage company and begin the process for removing PMI.

Removing PMI is nothing more than paying a marginal fee of about $350 and having a new appraisal done. With an FHA loan, MIP can't be removed until the loan itself is retired, either by paying off the mortgage or refinancing into a new loan that doesn't need mortgage insurance (MI).

Now let's look at that same scenario comparing a conventional with an FHA using 15 percent down.

	Conventional	FHA
Loan amount	$170,000	$170,000
MIP (FHA)		$2,975
Final loan amt	$170,000	$172,975
Payment	$965.24	$982
MI payment	54	71
Total with MI	$1,019	$1,053

You'll notice the total monthly payment dropped a bit more than the FHA loan. That's because with 15 percent down, conventional mortgage insurance requires less coverage while the FHA loan requirement stays the same at 0.25 percent of the loan amount.

Now let's figure this one more time using a 15-year instead of a 30-year fixed and the same 15 percent down.

	Conventional	FHA
Loan amount	$170,000	$170,000
MIP (FHA)		$2,975
Final loan amount	$170,000	$172,975
Payment	$1,389	$1,413
MI payment	93	0
Total with MI	$1,482	$1,413

A quirk in the FHA loan is that with 15 percent down, there is no monthly mortgage insurance premium, but there is still the initial upfront mortgage insurance premium of $2,975.

When borrowers consider putting 15 percent down instead of 20 percent, I suggest they evaluate the possibility of holding off and saving up the additional funds for a down payment. Again, with a $200,000 loan, 20 percent is $40,000 and 15 percent is $30,000.

Ten thousand dollars is certainly not a trivial amount, but for those who have the wherewithal to make a down payment large enough to avoid mortgage insurance, they should.

Why? For many, mortgage insurance is not a tax-deductible item. Unless you're a first-time homebuyer, the mortgage insurance monthly payment isn't tax deductible. You can't write it off like mortgage interest.

It may not sound fair to allow mortgage insurance deductibility only to a particular class, but you can bet mortgage insurance companies will keep trying to get that changed. Tax deductibility of mortgage insurance came about in the mid-2000s as a temporary inducement to first-time homebuyers who might have a problem saving up for a 20 percent down payment. One year after the temporary rule was enacted, the deductibility feature was made permanent.

You Might Now Be a First-Time Homeowner (Even if You Aren't)

An interesting feature of all first-time homebuyer loans is how a *first-timer* is actually defined. A first-timer must not have owned a home in the previous three years. That's it. One could have owned a home four years ago and still qualify for the mortgage interest tax deduction.

Here are two important notes that reflect new rules issued by mortgage insurance companies:

1. *Some mortgage insurance companies will not issue a policy if the loan was originated by a mortgage broker.* If you're using a mortgage broker and you have less than 20 percent down and may need mortgage insurance ask the broker if they have a source for mortgage insurance.

2. *Mortgage insurance companies may not issue policies for condominiums and townhomes if the down payment is less than 10 percent.* In essence, this eliminates mortgage insurance for condos and townhomes for anyone with little down. If the buyer has 10 percent down, then a piggyback loan would be the choice.

You Can Piggyback, Too

Another option for conventional loans with less than 20 percent down is by using a "piggyback," or second mortgage lien. In fact, before mortgage insurance became tax deductible, it was the preferred method of avoiding mortgage insurance. A borrower would take two mortgage loans; one at 80 percent of the sales price and a second mortgage based on the amount of down payment.

If the borrower had 15 percent down, the second mortgage would be 5 percent of the sales price. With 10 percent, the second mortgage would be 10 percent of the sales price, and with 5 percent down, the second mortgage would equal 15 percent of the sales price. A piggyback scenario looks like this—again, with the same $200,000 sales price, a 5.50 percent rate on the first and a 7.50 percent rate on the second, a common spread between a first and second mortgage.

80-15-5	(5 percent down)	Monthly Payment
First loan	$160,000	$908
Second loan	30,000	209
Total		$1,117

80-10-10	(10 percent down)	Monthly Payment
First loan	$160,000	$908
Second loan	20,000	139
Total		$1,047

The difference between total monthly payments is $70 per month. If you're not a first-time homebuyer and don't qualify for the mortgage insurance premium tax deduction and wanted to put less than 20 percent down, then you would want to structure a piggyback loan instead of paying mortgage insurance.

Say you do, however, qualify as a first-time homebuyer, how do the two scenarios stack up? With 10 percent down, the comparisons look like this:

80-10-10	Monthly Payment
First loan	$908
Second loan	$139
Total	$1,047

10 Percent Down with Mortgage Insurance	Monthly Payment
First loan	$1,022
MI payment	93
Total with MI	$1,115

In this comparison, the monthly payments for the 80–10–10 loan is $68 per month less, and the obvious choice is the 80–10–10 scenario.

As interest rates rise and fall, it is important to consider a loan with mortgage insurance versus a piggyback, as sometimes the choice might indeed be one with mortgage insurance. It would be the case if rates were higher than 5.50 percent and 7.50 percent. Say, rates were at 7.50 percent and 9.50 percent. The payments would then look like this:

80-10-10	Monthly Payment
First loan	$1,118
Second loan	$168
Total	$1,286

10 Percent Down with Mortgage Insurance	Monthly Payment
First loan	$1118
MI payment	93
Total with MI	$1,211

As mortgage rates rise, a loan with mortgage insurance can be the better choice, sometimes even without the added advantage of mortgage insurance deductibility. Mortgage insurance premiums are based on a set percentage and do not take into account current mortgage rate conditions.

If you've got 10 percent or more down and your loan amount is at or below current conforming loan limits, then the conventional loan is without a doubt your best choice.

VA LOANS

If you're qualified for a VA loan and have some down payment money, then it's not to your advantage to use your VA eligibility for a VA loan. Since every VA loan requires a funding fee of 2.15 percent, this gets added to your loan amount, wiping out that same amount you used as a down payment. If you had 20 percent down and your sales price was $300,000, then your down payment would be $60,000. The 2.15 percent funding fee adds up to $6,450, which is then added to your loan amount. Instead of your loan amount being $240,000 with a conventional loan, the VA loan amount would be $246,450. Comparing the interest paid over the life of each loan at 6.00 percent the interest charges would add up like this:

VA	$285,270
Conventional	$277,680

That's a difference in total interest paid of $7,590, not to mention the increase in monthly payment of $38. But if you do have little or nothing available for a down payment, then there is absolutely no comparison between a conventional, FHA, or USDA, and a VA. It's a VA loan. If you're VA eligible and want to learn more about VA mortgages in detail, I suggest reading my book *Your Guide to VA Home Loans*. Chapter 3 also has more information on VA loans.

FHA LOANS

If you don't have 10 percent or more down and you're not VA eligible, then you need to consider an FHA loan. Although FHA caters to first-time homebuyers more than any other class due to its lower down payment requirements, it's not just for first-timers. The only restrictions placed on FHA loans are the ones reserved for the maximum loan amounts, which can be found at HUD's website, https://entp.hud.gov/idapp/html/hicostlook.cfm. The drawback with FHA loans is that their limits are usually lower than their conventional cousins.

FHA loans are typically easier to qualify for in terms of credit and relaxed debt ratios when compared to a conventional loan. As pointed out in Chapter 3, while FHA loans do not have a minimum credit score, lenders in general have set the minimum credit score bar at 620.

FHA loans also carry two unique characteristics when compared to conventional as well as VA and USDA loans: source of down payment funds and nonoccupant co-borrowers.

FHA Loans Limit the Source of Down Payment Funds

For those fortunate ones who have relatives or another qualified entity with the ability and willingness to help financially with a down payment and closing costs, FHA should be strongly considered. Most often, these financial gifts come from immediate family members, but FHA does allow for other entities to provide financial gifts:

➤ Nonprofit organizations
➤ Churches/synagogues/religious institutions
➤ Government grants
➤ Life partners

Big Change: No More Seller-Assisted FHA Loans

One recent major change regarding gifts and FHA loans is the elimination of "seller assisted" down-payment funds. Because FHA requires gift funds to come from a family member or a nonprofit, for years companies were set up as a nonprofit for the sole purpose of facilitating an FHA purchase. It worked like this:

Buyers needed a 3 percent down payment to buy a $100,000 home but didn't have it. The seller could assist with the down payment but only by first giving it to the nonprofit set up to handle the gift. The seller would give the funds to the nonprofit, which would in turn send those funds to the closing agent. The nonprofit would charge a nominal fee.

In reality, this was nothing more than a loophole in the law. Sellers can't give buyers down payment funds. Sellers can contribute toward buyer closing costs but not toward down payment.

It was later discovered that these seller-assisted down payment arrangements carried a much higher default rate when compared to the same FHA loan where the buyers saved up their own money for the down payment or got the funds from a traditional nonprofit group. HUD ultimately made such transactions illegal, a significant ruling on a procedure that had grown in size and scope for the previous 10 years.

You May Only Need $500

A neat characteristic of FHA gifts is that the borrower only has to have a limited amount of funds in a purchase transaction. This minimum amount is just $500. By contrast, with a conventional loan that has a gift involved, the borrowers need to have 5 percent of their own funds in the down payment in addition to the gift. This requirement is waived only if the gift is 20 percent or more of the sales price. That means if the gift represents 5 or 10 percent of the sales price, then FHA is the way to go if the buyers have limited funds available.

Cosigning for Conventional Loans No Longer Makes Sense

FHA also has a unique advantage when additional qualifying income is needed. Sometimes borrowers need someone to cosign the mortgage to help them qualify from an income perspective. Usually, that means mom and dad agree to sign on the loan along with their kid.

While conventional loans allow for nonoccupant coborrowers, conventional loans still require the primary occupants, the borrowers, to qualify on their own without the additional income from their folks. This is a relatively recent change for conventional loans and negates the advantages of having a cosigner in the first place.

FHA loans don't have that requirement. The borrowers don't have to qualify on their own income, and in fact, don't have to have any income at all if the co-borrowers agree to cosign and can qualify based on their own income and current debt load.

You may have heard the term "kiddie condo." This is a term stemming from FHA loans, where the parents buy a house or condo but don't live there while putting their son or daughter on the note, as long as the son or daughter lives in the house or condo purchased. This is a common way for some parents to buy real estate for their child to live in while they attend college in lieu of renting an apartment or a house for four or more years.

USDA loans really have no peer, hence no competition. If the property is categorized as rural, there are little or no down payment funds available, and relaxed credit guidelines are required, then a USDA loan is the first choice.

CHOICE CHANGE: FIXED VERSUS ADJUSTABLE LOANS

Now that we've examined which type of loan program is best for you, let's consider another loan option: fixed rate or adjustable rate.

A fixed rate is easy to explain: The rate never, ever changes. Even if the loan is sold to another lender, the interest rate can never change. An adjustable rate takes a bit more explanation.

An adjustable rate mortgage, or ARM, has an interest rate that can vary throughout the term of the loan. It can go up, go down, or remain the same. But not randomly so, as the rules for rate adjustments are built into the mortgage.

Adjustable rate mortgages have three main characteristics:

1. Index
2. Margin
3. Caps

The index is the number that the mortgage is tied to. An index can be most anything that the mortgage describes but common indexes are the one-year Treasury bill or the prime rate, for example. Whatever the rate is on the one-year Treasury bill on the day your rate is to adjust, that's the index that will be used to help establish your rate.

The margin is the amount, in percent, that is added to the index to get your final interest rate. If the index is 5.00 percent and the margin is 2.50 percent, then 5.00 + 2.50 = 7.50 percent. Your interest rate on your adjustable rate mortgage would be 7.50 percent until your next adjustment.

Caps come in two varieties: interim and floor/ceiling. The interim cap is the maximum amount the rate can change at each adjustment. This helps protect the borrower from wild rate swings. Say, for instance, the prime rate the first year is 3.00 percent and the next year the prime is at 10.00 percent. With a margin of 2.50 percent, the first mortgage rate would be 3.00 + 2.50 = 5.50 percent. The following year, with the prime rate being 10.00 percent, the mortgage rate would be 10.00 + 2.50 = 12.50 percent.

On a $300,000 mortgage, that monthly payment difference is

staggering. On a 30-year fixed-rate term, 5.50 percent comes to $1,703, and the 12.50 percent rate gives us a $3,201 payment. Should the prime rate increase that dramatically, almost doubling the house payment, consumers could find themselves suddenly unable to pay the mortgage.

Caps limit the amount that the rate can go up or down at each adjustment to compensate for rate changes. Common caps are 1 percent every six months or 2 percent per year, and so on. There are also loans that have monthly caps as well, although those are typically reserved for second lien mortgages.

In the previous example, with a 2 percent annual cap, the rate wouldn't increase from 5.50 percent all the way to 12.50 percent, but would stop at 7.50 percent due to the 2.00 percent cap. The adjustment period is the point at which the rate can adjust. Most often, this adjustment period is six months or one year. Each year, for the life of the loan, the interest rate can change at the adjustment period based on the index and margin and capped at the appropriate level when necessary. The interest rate would then adjust to its new rate until the next adjustment period.

Caps are also put in place for the maximum and minimum, or floor, rate. These are called "lifetime" caps. Common lifetime caps are 6 percent above the initial, or start, rate. If the rate started out at 5.50 percent and the lifetime cap were 6 percent, then the highest the rate could ever go would be 5.50 + 6.00 = 11.50 percent.

Using the previous example, even if the rate added up to 12.50 percent, it would never get there because of the 6 percent lifetime cap. The floor rate is the lowest the rate could ever get. I've never seen floor rates below 3 percent, regardless of the index and margin.

Psst: There's a Cross Between a Fixed and an ARM

Another version of the ARM is called a hybrid. A hybrid is an ARM that is fixed for a predetermined number of years before turning into an ARM that adjusts every six months or every year.

Common hybrids are fixed for 3, 5, 7, and 10 years, then turn into an adjustable rate that adjusts either every six months or ever year. Hybrids are commonly noted as 3/1, 5/1, 7/1, and 10/1. A 3/1 ARM is fixed for three years and adjusts once per year. A 5/1 ARM is fixed for five years, and so on. For a hybrid that adjusts every six months, the notation is 3/6 or 5/6, for example. Hybrids have their own index, margins, and caps.

To ARM or Hybrid?

Primarily, you need to see where rates are when you're closing on a loan and how long you intend to keep the loan. ARMs can start out with artificially low *teaser rates*—rates below their true rate by adding the index and margin together. These teaser rates can be lower than what might currently be available with a fixed-rate loan.

Hybrids can also offer slightly more competitive rates than a fixed-rate loan but also just a tad higher than an ARM's teaser rate. A common spread might look like this:

ARM	4.00 percent
3/1	4.50 percent
30-year fixed	5.00 percent

Sometimes the interest rate markets act a bit odd and these spreads aren't so typical. One might find that an ARM or hybrid is nearly identical, or in some cases higher, than a fixed rate.

If, however, the spreads are similar to the ones just listed, then you might consider an ARM *if* you are short term and don't intend to keep the property very long or will otherwise retire the mortgage early by paying it off.

From a historical standpoint, it makes sense to take an adjustable rate mortgage when rates are at relative highs and to take fixed rates when rates are at or close to their lows. Interest rates move in cycles over the years. One of the better interest rate sites that I use is at www.hsh.com. By logging onto this website, you can research rates over the past 30 years. You can compare current market rates with historical ones to get an idea on where rates are in their cycle.

Negative Amortization Loans: You Can No Longer Find Them

Negative amortization loans is a complicated-sounding term that applies to adjustable rate mortgages and has essentially vanished. These loans have been around for the past 30 years and made their mark in the heydays of the early 1980s, when interest rates were at historical highs—as in 18 to 20 percent for a mortgage loan!

Negative amortization, or *neg-am loans,* are labeled such because the loan can actually increase rather than decrease when payments are made. That sounds odd, but neg-am loans give you a choice of how much to pay on your mortgage each month.

These loans were popular in the 1980s, essentially vanished in the 1990s, and reared their head again in the early 2000s, this time with a much more palatable moniker: *payment option arms.*

No matter what they're called, they're a bad deal, and they work like this:

You select a neg-am loan and it has three or four rate offerings each month: the contract rate, the fully indexed rate, interest only, or fixed and fully amortized.

The contract rate is the minimum amount you must pay, often as low as 1 percent. The fully indexed rate is the interest rate when the margin is added to the index as previously described. Interest only is simply paying the interest on the loan and none of the principal, which means the loan would never get paid down. And finally, the fixed and fully amortized rate is where the payment is fixed each and every month and paid off completely in a specified period.

A common neg-am loan might look similar to the following:

Loan amount	$300,000
Contract rate	1 percent
Fully indexed	5.50 percent
Fixed and amortized	6.00 percent

The neg-am is sometimes called the *pay option* because you in fact have choices, but not for very long. If you don't at least make the interest payment, your loan will grow; hence the term "negative amortization."

If you make only the contract rate of 1 percent, or $964 instead of the fully indexed payment of $1,873, then while the lender will let you do that, the difference between those payments is literally added back to the loan balance. In this instance, $909 is added back to your loan. If you continue to make only the contract rate payment, your loan will eventually grow to 110 percent of its original value, or in this example, $330,000.

When your loan grows to 110 percent of your original value, your loan changes into the fixed and fully amortized rate. Your mortgage payment would jump to $1,978 per month. Would you be able to afford that?

Neg-am loans can have their place when given to the right borrowers, such as someone who gets seasonal or irregular income and there's a choice between making a smaller payment every now and then when income is diminished.

Neg-am loans or payment option ARMs, whatever the name, should never be your choice for mortgage financing. Neg-am loans have now vanished, but as in the past, they tend to find their way back into the marketplace in one form or another.

LOAN TERMS

Another important consideration in choosing the right loan program for you is the actual loan term. Loan terms historically have been the standard 30-year fixed-rate loan. The loan starts and ends at preset dates and the payments never change. But there are other terms to consider as well. Why review various terms? Loans with longer terms require more interest to be paid, while loans with shorter terms ask for less in mortgage interest. But with a catch: The payments are higher. Sometimes they are much higher.

Loans can be amortized over 40 years, 30 years, 25 years, 20 years, 15 years, and 10 years. Let's take a quick look to see how the payments change as the loan term is shortened on a $300,000 loan at 6.00 percent.

Term	Payment
40 years	$1,650
30 years	$1,798
25 years	$1,932
20 years	$2,149
15 years	$2,531
10 years	$3,330

Notice that the 10-year loan payment is twice that of the 40-year rate! Now let's look at the amount of interest paid over the life of that same loan.

Term	Payment	Lifetime Interest
40 years	$1,650	$492,000
30 years	$1,798	$347,280
25 years	$1,932	$279,600
20 years	$2,149	$215,760
15 years	$2,531	$155,580
10 years	$3,330	$99,600

Although longer terms make for lower payments, the result is more interest paid over the life of the loan.

PREPAYMENT PENALTIES

Another major change in mortgage loans is the absence of prepayment penalties. Prepayment penalties are funds paid to the mortgage company if you pay anything extra on your mortgage in addition to the standard monthly payment. For instance, if you made a $2,000 payment and the standard payment is $1,000, then a prepayment penalty could be applied to the additional $1,000. For example, a lender could impose a 50 percent penalty to the additional $1,000 paid, which would result in just $500 being paid toward the loan balance and $500 to penalties instead of the entire $1,000 being applied to the loan balance.

Prepayment penalties have gone away with the subprime and alternative mortgage loans. And good riddance. Here's a trick: You can get a 30-year loan and treat it like a 15 (at your leisure). Because now you can get a 30-year fixed-rate loan and pay it as if it were a 25-, or 20- or 15-year loan, without the pressure of higher required monthly payments.

I find many of my clients selecting a 30-year loan and then making regular extra payments to pay the loan off sooner. That way, if some financial emergency occurred and the homeowner would feel pinched by making a higher payment, there is some breathing room. The homeowner would only make the 30-year payment and perhaps make the extra payment at a later date.

Is there any concrete advice about which term to take? Yes. Take the shortest term available that is also comfortable with your financial planning.

Using the previous example, if a 10-year payment of $3,330 is too much, although you'll save a significant amount of interest payments, then try the 15-year payment at $2,531. If that's too much still, then move to the 20-year plan, and so on.

What's comfortable? That depends on you, but lenders still use their own debt ratio guidelines, and typically the total monthly payment (PITI) should be around 30 percent of your gross monthly income. But that shouldn't be your own rule. If 30 percent sounds fine, then by all means go for it. If it sounds high, then lengthen the term, reduce your rate, or borrow less.

LOAN LIMITS

The next consideration is how much you're going to borrow, and this is limited by the loan limits established by the VA, Fannie and Freddie, USDA, and FHA. For instance, in Chapter 2, we discussed conventional loan limits being set at $417,000. This is a moving target, depending on which part of the country you're buying in. Larger metropolitan areas carry higher conventional limits compared to less populated, rural areas. Places like California and New York have areas where the median home price is much higher than in places such as Texas or Wyoming (http://www.fanniemae.com/aboutfm/loanlimits.jhtml). But what if the amount of money you need to borrow is above those limits? You can find what the current conventional limits are by visiting Go Jumbo.

Jumbo loans are defined as loan amounts above conforming and government limits. If the conforming limit is $417,000 in your area and you're borrowing $418,000, then you're going to be charged much higher rates than a conventional or government loan would charge, as explained in Chapter 2.

Avoid Jumbo Rates with a Piggyback

You can take the higher jumbo rates or you can use a piggyback mortgage to supplement your first mortgage loan. There are two loans with this method, a first and a second. By doing so, you'll secure lower overall rates and the subsequent payments that go along with them.

When the mortgage market imploded in the 2000s, piggyback

loans got their fair share of bad press. Piggyback loans were made to those who didn't have 20 percent of their own money for down payment. In fairness, as alternative and subprime loans expanded their market share, they began to include piggyback loans in their offerings. The toxic aspect of piggyback loans in the environment occurred when they were made to those with no down payment or tarnished credit or who could not document their income or assets. Piggyback loans did not mix well with alternative or subprime loans. The lenders who made those loans are no longer in business.

But over the past several decades, piggyback mortgages have taken a predominant and needed role in the mortgage lending industry. Properly placed of course. Here are a couple of ways to use a piggyback loan that will keep your payments lower and help you qualify for a jumbo mortgage.

Sales price	$500,000
Down payment	$50,000 (10 percent)
Loan amount	$450,000

Using a jumbo rate of 8.00 percent on $450,000 and a 30-year loan, the payment would be $3,301 per month. If you borrowed the market limit of $417,000 and used a conforming rate of 6.50 percent, the payment would be $2,635, a savings of $666 per month. But you had to come in with more than 10 percent down. You had to come in with not $50,000, but $83,000.

What if you didn't have that? Would you be forced to take the higher jumbo rate and payment? No. Consider the piggyback.

Sales price	$500,000
Down payment	$ 50,000 (10 percent)
Loan amount	$417,000
Second loan	$33,000

Now using two mortgages and with market rates, the payments would look like:

First loan at 6.50 percent $2,635
Second loan at 7.50 percent $230
Total $2,865

Jumbo mortgage at $450,000? $3,301. Piggyback? $2,865. You just saved $436 per month by using a piggyback. Next example, and with a higher loan amount:

Sales price $800,000
Down payment $160,000 (20 percent)
Loan amount $640,000

Monthly payment at 8.00 percent is $4,696. As jumbo rates are typically 1.0 to 1.5 percent higher than conforming conventional loans, the conforming rate would be 6.5 percent. But keeping the first mortgage at $417,000 with a 6.5 percent rate, the payment would be $2,635. Now add the second to make up the difference.

Sales price $800,000
Down payment $160,000 (20 percent)
Loan amount $417,000
Second loan $223,000

With a second loan rate at 7.50 percent, the payment works to $1,559. Add the first and second together, and the total payment is $4,194, or $502 less per month. Plus, since there are no prepayment penalties, one can pay down the second mortgage more aggressively than the first and eventually be left with one loan at the lower conforming rates.

You can find piggyback loans at most lenders, but most often they're issued by retail banks, separate and apart from the lender making the first mortgage. Regarding retail banks, they can sometimes offer yet another alternative: portfolio loans.

There Are Still Portfolio Loans; Just Harder to Find

Portfolio loans, loans that are issued but will remain in the bank's "portfolio," are loans that can be issued under almost any circumstance the bank deems worthy. These loans fall outside typical lending guidelines dictated by conventional and government rules.

Portfolio loans are usually reserved for jumbo loans and also either as ARMs or hybrids. There are even a few banks that operate wholesale divisions to help market these loans, but primarily, portfolio loans are issued by the original bank to one of its customers.

A portfolio loan might have a lower down payment requirement while negating the need for mortgage insurance or a piggyback. It could issue a loan program that requires only 10 percent down, no mortgage insurance with a maximum loan amount of say $900,000.

Banks don't underwrite portfolio loans to any universal standard because there's no secondary market they need to conform to. Banks may try and mimic each other's portfolio offerings if the mortgage seems popular with the consumer, but primarily the loan guidelines are, "What is the certainty we'll be paid back on time, every time?"

Portfolio lenders can't afford to make any mistakes. One or two bad portfolio loans can seriously affect a bank's viability and could even force a takeover by the FDIC. Portfolio loans are made to those with good credit, some down payment, and substantiated income.

Portfolio lending comes in cycles. When times are good, banks will be more likely to make a loan to one of their customers than when times are bad and money is tight. If you're in a situation where you don't fit the underwriting box of conventional and government loans, then you might try for portfolio lending at your local bank.

DOCUMENTATION

Documentation is the process where the lender collects third-party evidence that what you put in your loan application is true and correct. If you tell a lender you have good credit and you very well might—just don't think the lender won't pull an independent credit report to verify your claim. They most certainly will.

At the same time, the lender will collect information from your employer to verify your employment and review pay stubs to verify how much money you make and when you make it. Lenders can also review past income tax returns to verify income and look at bank or investment statements showing how much you have saved for a down payment and closing costs.

The documentation process can come in degrees of verification In the past, loans were documented and then reviewed by an underwriter. Now, the loan is put through the AUS before any evidence is collected. If the borrower has an excellent credit score of, say, anything above 740 and has 20 percent or more available for the down payment, then the documentation process will be less thorough than for someone with a 620 score and 5 percent down. Here are a few examples.

Income Must Be Documented

If you're a strong borrower, the loan will likely require only what is called a *verbal verification of employment,* or verbal VOE. With a verbal VOE, the lender looks up your employer's phone number and asks for the human resource department, and simply asks, "Does David Reed work there?" and, "When did he start?" The HR department will answer over the phone, and the lender enters the information on the verification form. The verbal VOE is then combined with a paycheck stub to verify the income.

That's it.

If you are not so strong a borrower, the lender would ask for last year's W-2, two most recent pay stubs covering 30 days, and a written VOE.

A written VOE is a form that is sent to the employer either by mail or fax or as an attachment in an e-mail. The employer completes the form and enters how long the person has worked there in addition to their pay structure.

The written VOE is then compared with the W-2s provided and the pay stubs. If there is any discrepancy the lender will need an explanation. For instance, if the pay stub says the borrower makes $5,000 per month but the W-2s only show $45,000 in income, something's not quite right: 12 months at $5,000 per month is $60,000, not $45,000. The lender needs an explanation. Perhaps the employee changed jobs or went from being a commission-earning salesperson to a salaried employee. Whatever the discrepancy, there must be a plausible and verifiable explanation.

If the borrower is self-employed and a strong borrower, the lender would likely only ask for a copy of last year's tax returns and use the income listed on the returns. If the borrower is self-employed and a weaker borrower, the lender might ask for two years of tax returns and perhaps a year-to-date profit and loss statement.

Lenders Require New Documentation from the IRS

The new guidelines also document income with a new method: the IRS form 4506T.

With the advent of software and computer technology, it's easier to fake a pay stub and even a W-2. Lenders can find themselves victims of fraudulent activity, all the while reviewing legitimate-looking documentation.

The 4506-T form is an IRS form that the borrowers sign and return to the lender upon application. This gives the lender permission to contact the IRS for copies of their previous year's tax returns and W-2s.

The form is faxed to the IRS, the IRS pulls the information (electronically) and the result of all that detective work takes about one to three days. When the returns and W-2s are forwarded to the lender, the lender compares the information supplied by the IRS with the information supplied by the borrower. This form is now required on all loans. Quite frankly, it should have always been the case to avoid the mortgage meltdown in the late 2000s.

Assets are also verified to evidence sufficient funds to close on a transaction. Again, strong borrowers might require less documentation than weaker borrowers. Strong borrowers might only require the most recent bank statement. Weaker borrowers might be asked to provide three months' worth of statements, plus a written verification of deposit, or VOD.

Lenders Now Verify Everything

This means there is no such thing as the stated documentation or "No doc" loans. Popular for years but really popular for those who couldn't or wouldn't document evidence of income, these loans required little, if any, documentation.

The borrowers would simply "state" on their loan application how much they made, and lenders would use that amount to underwrite the file. Needless to say, once some borrowers and crooked lenders got wind of the potential, it seemed nearly every other loan was stated or no doc. This makes sense, because in the mid-2000s, these loan types made up nearly 40 percent of the mortgage market.

Even now, I will still get the occasional phone call from someone who says, "I need a 'stated' loan; do you do those?" The answer, of course, is no, and neither does anyone else. And that's a good thing.

SUMMARY

> There are two primary types of mortgages; conventional and government-backed.

- If you have a down payment of 10 percent or more, you should strongly consider the conventional loan.
- If you're VA qualified and have no down payment, take the VA loan hands-down.
- If you're not qualified for VA and have little down, explore the FHA loan, making sure the amount you want to borrow doesn't exceed FHA's loan limits for your area.
- USDA loans are specifically designed for rural areas. If you have little or nothing down and live in a qualified rural area, USDA is the way to go.
- If you need a financial gift or someone to cosign for you, choose FHA.
- If you have enough money to put 20 percent down, do so.
- If you don't, then consider PMI or a piggyback.
- If you're a first-time homebuyer, both PMI and mortgage interest are tax deductible.
- If you're not a first-time homebuyer, only mortgage interest is tax deductible.
- Mortgage insurance may not work with mortgage brokers and may restrict first-timers.
- Lock in low fixed rates when rates are at historical lows.
- Consider ARMs and hybrids only if rates are at relative historical highs.
- Use a piggyback loan to avoid higher jumbo loan rates.
- Some banks still offer "outside the box" portfolio loans.
- Lenders no longer offer no doc or stated documentation loans. Everything is verified.

CHAPTER 7

Funds for Closing: Down Payments and Closing Costs

WITH THE DEMISE of the zero-down loan programs, HUD's ruling and subsequent banning of all seller-assisted down-payment loans, and all loans being fully documented for income, credit, and assets, it is become more difficult to qualify for a mortgage. In mine and many others' opinion, there's nothing really wrong with that. It's the way the mortgage industry has worked for more than 70 years. That, however, presents a problem when finding money to close on a purchase both in terms of down payments and for closing costs.

In this chapter, we'll discover how to save on closing costs, which ones are negotiable, and unique places to find down payment and closing cost money if you don't have enough money to close on a home.

CLOSING COSTS

The down payment, of course, is the amount of initial equity you put into the transaction, and unless you're VA or USDA qualified, that means a minimum of 3.5 percent down for an FHA loan or 5 percent down for a conventional one.

While borrowers initially think of how much money they need for a down payment, they sometimes forget or simply have no idea whatsoever on how much closing costs will be. And there will be a fair share of those. There are certain closing costs you must pay, ones you can negotiate, and ones that you won't pay at all.

Some Closing Costs Are Negotiable

Let's first break our closing costs down into two distinct areas; recurring and nonrecurring costs.

Nonrecurring fees are the one-time charges associated with obtaining a mortgage. Those fees are ones reserved for a credit report or an appraisal or perhaps an attorney. Recurring charges are ones that will happen again and again, way past your initial loan closing. Recurring charges are things such as property taxes, property insurance, and mortgage interest. You'll need to consider both when adding up how much money you'll need for closing costs.

Nonrecurring fees are also divided up into two areas: lender fees and nonlender fees. Lender fees are those the lender needs to evaluate the loan. Here are some common lender fees that you'll need to consider, and average amounts for each:

Origination fees	1.00% of the loan amount
Discount points	1.00% of the loan amount
Appraisal	$400
Credit report	$20
Inspection fees	$100
Mortgage broker fee	1% of the loan amount
Processing fee	$400
Tax service	$65
Underwriting	$500

That's a lot of fees. And we haven't even gotten to the nonlender fees—but before we do that, let's examine what each of them are for.

➤ *Origination fee.* Most often represented as a percentage of the loan amount, it's a common charge for mortgage brokers and mortgage lenders for part or all of their profit on the loan. Brokers get their loans on a wholesale basis, and by adding an origination fee, it brings the loan closer to retail.

This fee is commonly negotiable either in part or all, but only in exchange for an adjustment in rate. If you decide you want to pay points for a lower rate, you can do so, but conversely, if you agree to a higher rate, you can have that origination fee reduced or removed completely.

➤ *Discount point.* Represented as a percentage of the loan amount, it is the amount paid to lower, or "discount" the interest rate. Typically, you can pay one point and reduce your rate by 0.25 percent. Like origination fees, you may also increase your interest rate on your loan and reduce or eliminate the discount point.

This fee is also negotiable, depending on the rate you select.

➤ *Appraisal.* Not negotiable unless you can work a deal with your loan officer to pay for it themselves. The appraisal is a written report, with pictures, that attempts to determine the current market value of real estate. In a purchase transaction the appraisal supports the sales price and in a refinance the appraisal helps to determine maximum loan amounts.

➤ *Credit report.* Easy enough to understand, it's the cost of obtaining your credit report from the credit reporting agencies. Lenders and mortgage brokers can't use a credit report provided by you; they'll order one directly for themselves. Credit report fees typically aren't negotiable.

➤ *Inspection fees.* There are two types of inspection fees, one during construction where the bank sends an inspector to the home being built to check on the progress and another type of inspection that evaluates the current physical condition of the property such as cracked walls, old wiring, or a roof that is in bad shape.

Inspection fees can't typically be waived and are paid up front.

➤ *Mortgage broker fee.* If a mortgage broker doesn't charge you an origination fee, sometimes they put their fees in this column. If you're getting charged both, I'd ask some questions; you shouldn't be paying both. This fee should also be negotiable.

➤ *Processing fee.* A lender charge that covers the initial overhead of processing the loan. Loan processing is the physical act of documenting a loan file to be sent to an underwriter. This loan might be negotiable, but if it's waived it's the loan officer paying for it out of her own pocket.

➤ *Tax service.* Lenders pay tax-service companies a fee to monitor the payment of property taxes. If the property taxes aren't being paid by the borrower, the lender will typically pay them on behalf of the borrower and then demand immediate reimbursement from the homeowner.

➤ *Underwriting.* Another lender charge that covers the cost of making sure the loan meets loan guidelines. Typically, this is not negotiable, as the underwriter gets paid from those funds.

One Way to Save on Appraisals: Wait!

One way that you may be able to save money on an appraisal is to wait and see what the AUS said in its approval. Many times with 20 percent down and good credit, the AUS won't require a full-blown appraisal costing somewhere around $400. Sometimes you can get a reduced appraisal type called a "drive-by" where the property isn't physically inspected, just compared to local sales. This can save you about $200. Regardless, ask your loan officer if your AUS allows for a cheaper appraisal.

Jumbo loans and government loans can be more expensive than $400. Loans over $650,000 often require two appraisals. With the new HVCC appraisal guidelines, you will be asked to give a credit or debit card number to an appraisal management group, who will order the appraisal for you.

The HVCC rules will also ask for a brand new appraisal should you decide to change lenders. This controversial ruling riled mortgage brokers, but in reality, it will likely only have them concentrate more on finding you the best deal instead of simply shopping your loan package all over town.

Some Closing Costs Are Nonnegotiable

Third-party fees, fees not attributed to your lender, are almost all nonnegotiable. You might be able to contact directly the attorney on your transaction and ask for various discounts or see if you can get any breaks on title insurance, but often such fees are regulated by state law.

You may find that title insurance and title-related fees are set by the insurance commission in your state where you live and can't offer discounts. Other than someone paying such fees for you, the charge rarely can be negotiated lower. Here are some common non-lender closing costs you are likely to encounter:

> *Closing or escrow fee.* This is the amount paid to the person or company who is handling your closing at the closing table. This person makes sure all the closing papers are drawn and signed properly, manages the funds coming from the buyer to the seller, and follows any specific instructions from the lender required to close the loan. $350 is a common amount.

> *Flood certificate.* This is a standard charge on every loan that pulls a report from the Federal Emergency Management Agency, or FEMA, noting whether the property in question is in a flood zone. If it is, your insurance will be much higher than if it is not in a flood zone, sometimes as much as three times more expensive. Tax service charges are not negotiable.

➤ *Document preparation fee.* A fee is charged to review and print closing papers to be delivered to your closing agent. The fee is usually around $200.

➤ *Attorney fees.* This depends a lot on where you hold your closing. In California, for instance, no attorneys are involved unless the buyer or seller employ them to review their various documents. In other states such as Illinois, attorneys are the entities that handle closing; while in Texas, all mortgage loan documents must be reviewed by attorneys. The cost is typically $200 to $500.

➤ *Title insurance.* Title insurance is an insurance policy that protects the lender and the owner from previous claims to the property and assures that all previous sales of the property were handled in a legal, enforceable way.

➤ *Recording fees.* Government fees cover the cost of recording the real estate transaction in public records. This is typically $50 to $200.

These aren't all the fees you might encounter, but generally speaking, you'll find these fees in most parts of the country. Non-lender fees usually can't be negotiated at all. Why would an attorney work for free or reduce the charges when he doesn't have to?

FEE DISCLOSURE

How do you find out about all these various fees? Your loan officer is required by law to disclose these fees to you immediately if the loan officer takes your application face to face or within three business days after receiving your application via mail, fax, or the Internet.

This required disclosure is given to you by way of the good faith estimate of settlement charges, or simply good faith or GFE. This is a confusing form, with each potential charge assigned a number. The origination fee is always entered on line 801, for instance. The attorney fee is entered on line 1107.

New Regulations Prevent Surprises at the Closing Table

The GFE was inherently confusing as well as misleading—terms that most consumers have never used before, line item numbers that don't seem to make sense, and overall a page full of dizzying words and dollars signs. Exhibit 7–1 s a typical GFE.

Consumers could go into a closing and expect to pay $5,000 in closing costs, only to find out that the number was closer to $7,000. When you go to a closing and you disagree with the closing costs, you're typically stuck by either paying those fees or losing both your earnest money deposit as well as the home.

Here's an example of what was quoted on the initial GFE and what could be seen at the settlement table for a $300,000 loan.

801	Origination fee	–o–
802	Discount point	–o–
803	Appraisal fee	$400
804	Credit report	$20
808	Mortgage broker fee	–o–
810	Processing	$400
811	Underwriting fee	$500
812	Flood certificate	$50
Total lender charges		$1,370

A couple of weeks later, when you go to your closing, you find the following staring at you in the face:

801	Origination fee	$3,000
802	Discount point	$3,000
803	Appraisal fee	$400
804	Credit report	$20
808	Mortgage broker fee	–o–
810	Processing	$400
811	Underwriting fee	$500
812	Flood certificate	$50
Total lender charges		$7,370

Exhibit 7-1. Good faith estimate.

Applicants:
Property Addr:
Prepared By:

Application No:
Date Prepared:
Loan Program:

The information provided below reflects estimates of the charges which you are likely to incur at the settlement of your loan. The fees listed are estimates-actual charges may be more or less. Your transaction may not involve a fee for every item listed. The numbers listed beside the estimates generally correspond to the numbered lines contained in the HUD-1 settlement statement which you will be receiving at settlement. The HUD-1 settlement statement will show you the actual cost for items paid at settlement.

Total Loan Amount $ Interest Rate: %   Term: mths

800	ITEMS PAYABLE IN CONNECTION WITH LOAN:	PFC	S	F	POC
801	Loan Origination Fee	$			
802	Loan Discount				
803	Appraisal Fee				
804	Credit Report				
805	Lender's Inspection Fee				
808	Mortgage Broker Fee				
809	Tax Related Service Fee				
810	Processing Fee				
811	Underwriting Fee				
812	Wire Transfer Fee				

1100	TITLE CHARGES:	PFC	S	F	POC
1101	Closing or Escrow Fee		$		
1105	Document Preparation Fee				
1106	Notary Fees				
1107	Attorney Fees				
1108	Title Insurance				

1200	GOVERNMENT RECORDING & TRANSFER CHARGES:	PFC	S	F	POC
1201	Recording Fees		$		
1202	City/County Tax/Stamps				
1203	State Tax/Stamps				

1300	ADDITIONAL SETTLEMENT CHARGES:	PFC	S	F	POC
1302	Pest Inspection		$		

Estimated Closing Costs

900	ITEMS REQUIRED BY LENDER TO BE PAID IN ADVANCE:	PFC	S	F	POC
901	Interest for _____ days @ $ _____ per day		$		
902	Mortgage Insurance Premium				
903	Hazard Insurance Premium				
904					
905	VA Funding Fee				

(continued)

Exhibit 7-1. Good faith estimate. (continued)

1000	RESERVES DEPOSITED WITH LENDER:			PFC	S	F	POC
1001	Hazard Insurance Premiums	months @ $	per month	$			
1002	Mortgage Ins. Premium Reserves	months @ $	per month				
1003	School Tax	months @ $	per month				
1004	Taxes and Assessment Reserves	months @ $	per month				
1005	Flood Insurance Reserves	months @ $	per month				
		months @ $	per month				
		months @ $	per month				

Estimated Prepaid Items/Reserves

TOTAL ESTIMATED SETTLEMENT CHARGES

TOTAL ESTIMATED FUNDS NEEDED TO CLOSE:			TOTAL ESTIMATED MONTHLY PAYMENT:	
Purchase Price/Payoff (+)		New First Mortgage(-)	Principal & Interest	
Loan Amount (-)	0.00	Sub Financing(-)	Other Financing (P & I)	
Est. Closing Costs (+)	0.00	New 2nd Mtg Closing Costs(+)	Hazard Insurance	
Est. Prepaid Items/Reserves (+)	0.00		Real Estate Taxes	
Amount Paid by Seller (-)			Mortgage Insurance	
			Homeowner Assn. Dues	
			Other	

| Total Est. Funds needed to close | | 0.00 | Total Monthly Payment |

These estimates are provided pursuant to the Real Estate Settlement Procedures Act of 1974, as amended (RESPA). Additional information can be found in the HUD Special Information Booklet, which is to be provided to you by your mortgage broker or lender, if your application is to purchase residential real property and the lender will take a first lien on the property.   The undersigned acknowledges receipt of the booklet "Settlement Costs," and if applicable the Consumer Handbook on ARM Mortgages.

_____   _____   _____   _____
Applicant   Date   Applicant   Date

What should you do? Why, you call that rascally loan officer and tell him you're not paying—and he tells you that he had already discussed those fees with you and you had better take it or leave it.

You call your agent, you call your attorney, and you call anyone you think can help. But even though GFEs were required, there was no enforcement mechanism to punish the bad guys, nor any threshold that would trigger any such enforcement.

You were stuck. So you decided to grit your teeth and pay the extra money and sue the loan officer later.

That potential nightmare has gone away. New guidelines require the closing costs be no more than 10 percent higher when compared with the most recent GFE signed by the borrower. This is done when a lender gets ready to order the final closing papers to send to the settlement agent. The lender will review the fees listed in the loan documents and then compare them to the GFE that is in the loan file.

If the fees are higher, the lender won't print closing documents until it receives an updated GFE showing the higher loan charges with the borrowers' signature. In reality, this has always been the case with scrupulous loan officers. It's the unscrupulous ones that always cause the problems.

In addition to requiring loan documents to reflect the initial good faith estimate, lenders are now required to prepare and more consumer-friendly version of the good faith that describes not just potential charges, but other key features of the loan, such as adjustment periods if the loan is an ARM or if the loan carries any balloon feature. The new form (see Exhibit 7–2) even explains things in language most anyone can understand.

New GFE Uses Language You Can Understand

This new GFE is divided into three sections, but you'll notice that the biggest change is that along with the fee itself, there is a description in language you can understand.

Exhibit 7-2. New good faith estimate.

OMB Approval No. 2502-0265

Good Faith Estimate (GFE)

Name of Originator	Borrower
Originator Address	Property Address
Originator Phone Number	
Originator Email	Date of GFE

Purpose

This GFE gives you an estimate of your settlement charges and loan terms if you are approved for this loan. For more information, see HUD's *Special Information Booklet* on settlement charges, your *Truth-in-Lending Disclosures*, and other consumer information at www.hud.gov/respa. If you decide you would like to proceed with this loan, contact us.

Shopping for your loan

Only you can shop for the best loan for you. Compare this GFE with other loan offers, so you can find the best loan. Use the shopping chart on page 3 to compare all the offers you receive.

Important dates

1. The interest rate for this GFE is available through ⬚⬚⬚⬚⬚. After this time, the interest rate, some of your loan Origination Charges, and the monthly payment shown below can change until you lock your interest rate.

2. This estimate for all other settlement charges is available through ⬚⬚⬚⬚⬚.

3. After you lock your interest rate, you must go to settlement within ⬚ days (your rate lock period) to receive the locked interest rate.

4. You must lock the interest rate at least ⬚ days before settlement.

Summary of your loan

Your initial loan amount is	$
Your loan term is	years
Your initial interest rate is	%
Your initial monthly amount owed for principal, interest, and any mortgage insurance is	$ per month
Can your interest rate rise?	☐ No ☐ Yes, it can rise to a maximum of %. The first change will be in .
Even if you make payments on time, can your loan balance rise?	☐ No ☐ Yes, it can rise to a maximum of $
Even if you make payments on time, can your monthly amount owed for principal, interest, and any mortgage insurance rise?	☐ No ☐ Yes, the first increase can be in and the monthly amount owed can rise to $. The maximum it can ever rise to is $.
Does your loan have a prepayment penalty?	☐ No ☐ Yes, your maximum prepayment penalty is $.
Does your loan have a balloon payment?	☐ No ☐ Yes, you have a balloon payment of $ due in years.

Escrow account information

Some lenders require an escrow account to hold funds for paying property taxes or other property-related charges in addition to your monthly amount owed of $⬚.

Do we require you to have an escrow account for your loan?

☐ No, you do not have an escrow account. You must pay these charges directly when due.

☐ Yes, you have an escrow account. It may or may not cover all of these charges. Ask us.

Summary of your settlement charges

A	Your Adjusted Origination Charges *(See page 2.)*	$
B	Your Charges for All Other Settlement Services *(See page 2.)*	$
A + B	Total Estimated Settlement Charges	$

**derstanding
ur estimated
ttlement charges**

Your Adjusted Origination Charges

1. **Our origination charge**
   This charge is for getting this loan for you.

2. **Your credit or charge (points) for the specific interest rate chosen**
   - ☐ The credit or charge for the interest rate of [____] % is included in "Our origination charge." (See item 1 above.)
   - ☐ You receive a credit of $[_____] for this interest rate of [____] %. This credit **reduces** your settlement charges.
   - ☐ You pay a charge of $[_____] for this interest rate of [____] %. This charge (points) **increases** your total settlement charges.

   The tradeoff table on page 3 shows that you can change your total settlement charges by choosing a different interest rate for this loan.

A | Your Adjusted Origination Charges | $

Your Charges for All Other Settlement Services

*ne of these charges
change at settlement.
the top of page 3 for
re information.*

3. **Required services that we select**
   These charges are for services we require to complete your settlement. We will choose the providers of these services.
   Service   *Charge*

4. **Title services and lender's title insurance**
   This charge includes the services of a title or settlement agent, for example, and title insurance to protect the lender, if required.

5. **Owner's title insurance**
   You may purchase an owner's title insurance policy to protect your interest in the property.

6. **Required services that you can shop for**
   These charges are for other services that are required to complete your settlement. We can identify providers of these services or you can shop for them yourself. Our estimates for providing these services are below.
   Service   *Charge*

7. **Government recording charges**
   These charges are for state and local fees to record your loan and title documents.

8. **Transfer taxes**
   These charges are for state and local fees on mortgages and home sales.

9. **Initial deposit for your escrow account**
   This charge is held in an escrow account to pay future recurring charges on your property and includes ☐ all property taxes, ☐ all insurance, and ☐ other [_____].

10. **Daily interest charges**
    This charge is for the daily interest on your loan from the day of your settlement until the first day of the next month or the first day of your normal mortgage payment cycle. This amount is $[____] per day for [____] days (if your settlement is [_____]).

11. **Homeowner's insurance**
    This charge is for the insurance you must buy for the property to protect from a loss, such as fire.
    Policy   *Charge*

B | Your Charges for All Other Settlement Services | $

A + **B** | Total Estimated Settlement Charges | $

 Good Faith Estimate (HUD-GFE) 2

(continued)

Instructions

Understanding which charges can change at settlement

This GFE estimates your settlement charges. At your settlement, you will receive a HUD-1, a form that lists your actual costs. Compare the charges on the HUD-1 with the charges on this GFE. Charges can change if you select your own provider and do not use the companies we identify. (See below for details.)

These charges **cannot increase** at settlement:	The total of these charges **can increase up to 10%** at settlement:	These charges **can change** at settlement:
■ Our origination charge ■ Your credit or charge (points) for the specific interest rate chosen *(after you lock in your interest rate)* ■ Your adjusted origination charges *(after you lock in your interest rate)* ■ Transfer taxes	■ Required services that we select ■ Title services and lender's title insurance *(if we select them or you use companies we identify)* ■ Owner's title insurance *(if you use companies we identify)* ■ Required services that you can shop for *(if you use companies we identify)* ■ Government recording charges	■ Required services that you can shop for *(if you do not use companies we identify)* ■ Title services and lender's title insurance *(if you do not use companies we identify)* ■ Owner's title insurance *(if you do not use companies we identify)* ■ Initial deposit for your escrow account ■ Daily interest charges ■ Homeowner's insurance

Using the tradeoff table

In this GFE, we offered you this loan with a particular interest rate and estimated settlement charges. However:

■ If you want to choose this same loan with **lower settlement charges,** then you will have a **higher interest rate.**
■ If you want to choose this same loan with a **lower interest rate,** then you will have **higher settlement charges.**

If you would like to choose an available option, you must ask us for a new GFE.

Loan originators have the option to complete this table. Please ask for additional information if the table is not completed.

	The loan in this GFE	The same loan with lower settlement charges	The same loan with a lower interest rate
Your initial loan amount	$	$	$
Your initial interest rate¹	%	%	%
Your initial monthly amount owed	$	$	$
Change in the monthly amount owed from this GFE	No change	You will pay $ **more** every month	You will pay $ **less** every month
Change in the amount you will pay at settlement with this interest rate	No change	Your settlement charges will be **reduced** by $	Your settlement charges will **increase** by $
How much your total estimated settlement charges will be	$	$	$

¹ For an adjustable rate loan, the comparisons above are for the initial interest rate before adjustments are made.

Using the shopping chart

Use this chart to compare GFEs from different loan originators. Fill in the information by using a different column for each GFE you receive. By comparing loan offers, you can shop for the best loan.

	This loan	Loan 2	Loan 3	Loan 4
Loan originator name				
Initial loan amount				
Loan term				
Initial interest rate				
Initial monthly amount owed				
Rate lock period				
Can interest rate rise?				
Can loan balance rise?				
Can monthly amount owed rise?				
Prepayment penalty?				
Balloon payment?				
Total Estimated Settlement Charges				

If your loan is sold in the future

Some lenders may sell your loan after settlement. Any fees lenders receive in the future cannot change the loan you receive or the charges you paid at settlement.

 Good Faith Estimate (HUD-GFE) 3

The first section is consumer information that describes what the GFE actually is and how to use it to compare different lenders. It gives a basic summary of your loan, such as your loan amount, your loan term, your initial interest rate, and your monthly payments.

And instead of simply showing whether you have an ARM, there is a question that asks: Can your interest rate rise? Yes or No.

If it is yes, then it describes the various change dates, index, and margin.

The second section is the Summary of Settlement Charges and is divided into sections A and B.

Section A is for the *adjusted origination charges,* which are any origination charges or discount points for a selected interest rate. As rates move and as you can choose a lower rate by paying more, this section helps to explain the rate/point relationship.

Section B is for "all other" charges for settlement services, which include title insurance, recording, and any other third-party fees.

Finally, the last section gives you a chart to help you compare different loan offerings from different lenders.

This new GFE is the first major change in explaining settlement services in nearly two decades. It's a typical government effort in that sometimes to try explaining things it can explain too much. The new GFE is three pages long, for instance, and the old one was one page.

It would have been better to keep the old GFE and have the loan officer take the time to explain each item, rather than place the burden on the consumer. It's also interesting to note that this new government form encourages consumers to shop around for the best terms by literally placing a comparison chart for the consumer to use right in the GFE itself. But unless the consumer knows the correct way to negotiate through all the various closing costs, it will be a wasted effort.

Psst: The Fed Doesn't Set Your Mortgage Rate

The most important part of your GFE is the interest rate. After all, what you're really looking for is the best rate, right? Know that the

GFE is not very trustworthy until you've selected a lender and locked in a rate. But rates can move throughout the day. One common misperception is that the Fed controls your mortgage rate, when that's simply not the case. Mortgage rates are tied to a bond—specifically, a mortgage bond.

The Fed's job is to control inflation, or the cost of money. It does that by raising or lower the cost of money to banks, which, in turn, lend it to consumers. When you hear on the news that the Fed reduced rates by a quarter percent, for example, what it actually lowered is the Federal Funds rate. This is the rate set by the Fed that banks can charge one another for short-term loans.

Banks have reserve requirements, meaning they have to have enough cash in their vaults somewhere to cover all their obligations just in case all their customers decided to line up at their window and withdraw all their deposits, as they did in the bank runs at the beginning of the Great Depression.

That means that when banks make a loan to someone, they have to make sure they still have enough money in their required reserves. If a bank loans $10 million, then it has to have $10 million less in reserves. If it doesn't have enough money in reserves, it has to borrow from another bank to meet its reserve requirements.

The Fed acts to stimulate or slow down an economy. When the economy is moving at break-neck speed, the unemployment rate goes way down and everyone starts buying stuff. All three of these indicate a booming economy and the likelihood of inflation.

When the Fed sees that inflation might be a problem, it can raise the Fed Funds rate. When it costs more for banks to borrow money, they then raise the rates they charge their consumers. If it costs more for consumers to borrow money, they might have second thoughts about buying that new car, buying that new house, or starting a new business.

The Fed meets every six weeks and looks at recent, current, and projected economic conditions to decide what to do with rates. In this situation, the Fed would raise rates to slow down the economy. Or, the economy is simply plugging right along, doing well but not extremely well, and the unemployment rate is holding steady. At the next Fed meeting, it would likely decide to keep rates the same.

In a sluggish economy, the Fed will lower rates to encourage borrowing, as low as zero percent if necessary. Since rates are tied to a mortgage bond, how does the Fed influence interest rates? Sometimes it has no influence, but Fed moves give an indication on how it thinks the economy will be doing in the future and if there are any signs of inflation.

Inflation is the archenemy of any bond, including mortgage bonds. As you know, bonds give a set return over a predetermined period. If you bought a $10 bond for $7 that matured in five years, after five years that $7 turns into $10.

But inflation will devalue a currency, and if inflation hits say, 10 percent, then after five years that $10 would be worth less than what it was originally purchased for.

Okay, enough of that. It is important to understand how rates move but more important to know that all mortgage lenders set their interest rate on the very same bond and track that bond throughout the day.

Compare Apples to Apples (to Get the Best Deal)

A 30-year conventional loan would be tied to a Fannie bond, for instance. As the bond improves in performance that trading day, rates will be lower. If the bond loses value because of fears of inflation, rates will go up to compensate for the loss in the bonds value.

This is why one lender can't be at 6.00 percent and everyone else is at 7.00 percent. If you get a lender with an unheard-of interest rate that is 0.25 percent or more lower than everyone else, either the loan officer is doing a free loan or the loan officer is misleading you. I'd guess the latter. Because rates can be had in eighth-percent increments, the resultant YSP will also change, and so can any potential points, origination fees, or broker fees. With that in mind, here are the key points to remember when getting interest rate quotes from different lenders.

- ➤ Decide up front the loan terms you want.
- ➤ Get your rates quoted to you at the same time of day.
- ➤ Ask for the accompanying lender fees for that loan.
- ➤ Get the rate quote for an exact period of time.

Decide Up Front the Loan Terms You Want

It's hard enough to compare a 30-year fixed rate at 6.00 percent and 6.125 percent. It's nearly impossible to compare a 30-year with a 25-year, a 20-year, and so on. Ask for the loan quote for one term, not a range.

It's also much easier for a loan officer to confuse you with different loan terms. In the previous chapter we discussed how to select the proper loan, so don't let a loan officer change your mind. It's possible that a loan officer might be able to make another $500 in YSP if you took a 15-year loan and not a 30-year. The rate might be a little lower as well, making the 15-year loan seem more attractive.

Or a loan officer might not be as competitive on a 20-year so he tries to get you to switch to a 25-year loan. Most loan officers get paid on commission. No loans, no paychecks. Some can get fairly aggressive when it comes to getting a loan from a consumer. Hold your ground and you'll be fine. Don't be tempted to consider any suggestions from the loan officer after you've made your original loan choice.

Get Your Rates Quoted to You at the Same Time of Day

Rates move, and sometimes they can move wildly. I've seen rates change by as much as a quarter percent in one day, most often to the worse. When you begin making phone calls or sending out e-mails to get rate quotes, make sure you do it at the same time of day to avoid any rate variance that can occur during the day.

This is also a major reason not to consider any interest rates you see quoted in the newspaper or on the Internet. Rates in the print media are already days old, and even rates on the Internet can be old. Lenders who rely solely on advertising their ultra-low interest rates must have a business model that doesn't revolve around establishing relationships with local real estate agents, accountants, attorneys, or anyone who might be a good referral source for potential borrowers.

Ask for the Accompanying Lender Fees for That Loan

Do this correctly; don't simply ask for closing costs. We've discussed this in depth because it is the most important consideration when shopping around for rates and comparing different loan offerings.

Get the Rate Quote for an Exact Period of Time

Because interest rates move, you need to get that rate guaranteed to you, or locked in. If you simply asked for a rate without specifying how long you'd need the money for, you're likely to get a shorter-term quote.

Rates that are good for only 7 days, for instance, will be lower than rates for 30 days. If you've got a contract that closes within 30 days, make sure you get a rate quote that will protect you for 30 days.

If your loan won't close for 60 days or beyond, your rate will be even higher. Some lenders even ask for a 1 percent commitment fee up front to lock in loans for longer periods.

With all that in mind, your message to the loan officer will go something like this:

"What is your rate with no points and one origination fee for my loan amount of $200,000? I need a 15-year loan for 30 days. I also need all the lender fees as well."

If you did this around the same time of day, you did it perfectly.

IMPORTANT CHANGES: INTEREST RATE LOCKS

Rates quoted over the phone however may not be available to you, you've just identified the more competitive lender.

A rate lock is serious business with a lender. When you request that your lender lock in your rate, the lender reserves enough money from its funds at the rate you selected. If your loan doesn't close with the lender, it loses money.

If a broker locks in your loan and you don't close, the broker may soon find itself in hot water with its wholesale lenders. Too many "blown locks" with a wholesale lender will likely lead to the wholesale lender removing that broker from its approved broker list.

It used to be a common practice for a consumer to apply at different lenders, lock at one of them, and wait to see how the market did. Lenders didn't like that, but there wasn't a whole lot the lender could do. Eventually, however, the lenders decided to pay more attention to their cost of doing business as well as their marketing plans. Some companies, most of them now out of business, would advertise something like, "Lock and Shop," which would allow a consumer to lock in a mortgage loan without even having a property or even paying any money to the lender.

This practice eventually went away, primarily because the lenders were bleeding money via blown locks. Consumers found a loophole and exploited it.

Now, lenders or mortgage brokers won't take lock requests unless they have your loan application in their possession. They also may not lock in your loan unless you're approved with them. Further, they may not lock in your loan unless you've paid an application fee or paid for an appraisal.

To lock in a rate, be prepared to commit to the lender as your lender of choice and stop the rate shopping. When you lock, your rate is guaranteed should rates rise. What if rates go down after you lock? You're out of luck, pretty much. When lenders lock you in, they reserve money for you at the terms you requested. If rates go up, they're not going to call you and ask you if it's okay if they raise your rate, since rates are higher.

Conversely, they won't do much if rates go down and you call and ask for the lower rates after you already locked in. Besides, if you've got a purchase contract closing on the thirtieth and it's the fifteenth, that's not enough time to threaten to move your loan to another lender.

You do hold more sway if your loan request is for a refinance. If you have an application approved and locked in at, say, 6.0 percent, and rates drop to 5.5 percent everywhere else, you can then threaten to move your loan to another lender. You can also expect a phone call from a good loan officer who didn't get your original quote saying, "Hey David. I was wondering if you locked in with another lender. Our rates today are a full one half percent better than what I had two weeks ago."

If the lender has already approved your loan and you're simply waiting for the loan to move through the process, you have the luxury of closing when you want to close. I discuss how to properly refinance a mortgage in my book *An Insider's Guide to Refinancing Your Mortgage.*

 Time is on your side. It can also be to your detriment.

Say that you're considering a refinance because rates dropped to 5 percent and your rate is at 7 percent and your mortgage balance is $250,000. Your current payment is $1,663 per month but could drop to $1,342 per month with the new 5 percent rate. That's over $300 in savings. But I've seen people over my career make a damaging mistake: holding out for just one more rate drop.

I recall a client who could have saved over $200 per month by refinancing to the lower market rates. He had a rate goal in mind; he wanted to get 4.75 percent. Rates had dropped to 5 percent and his monthly payment would have dropped over $200 immediately, but he kept holding out, waiting for that move to 4.75 percent. The difference between the 5.00 percent that was available and the 4.75 percent was $38. The problem was that he began to get greedy and waited and waited for his target rate. He waited four months until his target rate became available, and he locked.

The problem with his strategy? For those four months, he could have saved nearly $900, but instead chose to wait out for an additional $38 per month. If you divide $900 by $38 the answer is 23.7. He would have to wait another two years to see the benefits of waiting for that extra $38 per month.

On the flip side? Rates don't have to cooperate with you. Rates could have just as easily moved up to 6.00 percent, and he would have permanently lost any gains he could have acquired by locking in at 5.00 percent. No one can predict the future.

Time during a refinance can indeed be your friend or your foe.

I have literally closed thousands of mortgage loans. I have been asked. "Do you think I should lock?" countless times. I've never given an answer one way or the other. I've never been a fan of telling someone to lock in, then see rates drop, or tell them they shouldn't lock in and see rates go up.

But what I do say is this: Assume that whatever decision you make will be the wrong one. If you lock and rates go down, hey, you got the market rates just like everybody else did. If you didn't lock and rates shoot up, you're paying for that decision for as long as you own that mortgage, and you'll be reminded of it on the first of each month." Lock. Sleep at night.

That's how rates are set and that's how lenders treat those rates. But you're not done.

NEGOTIATING CLOSING FEES WITH THE LENDER

You need to now negotiate your closing fees from your various rate quotes.

How do you correctly negotiate these fees from different lenders? If you're not careful with this new GFE, you can get confused. Remember the difference between lender and nonlender charges? If you don't keep those separate while comparing GFEs from different lenders, you might not get your best deal.

Here are the lender charges, again using the old GFE:

801	Origination fee	–o–
802	Discount point	–o–
803	Appraisal fee	$400
804	Credit report	$20
808	Mortgage broker fee	–o–
810	Processing	$400
811	Underwriting fee	$500
812	Flood certificate	$50
	Total lender charges	$1,370

These are the fees you should be concerned with when comparing lenders, and no others. At least from a comparative standpoint.

If you just ask for the total amount for closing costs, lender as well as nonlender, loan officers can lowball the third-party fees and there's not much you can do about it. Lenders have no control over title insurance or attorney fees or recording charges, but they are the ones that prepare the GFE for you to review. That means they can lower the nonlender fees to make their overall package look better.

It's critical to make your own worksheet when comparing GFEs with two columns labeled "lender" and "nonlender."

One final point regarding the new GFE is regarding the YSP, or *yield spread premium.* YSPs, a function of a higher rate, are funds that are available from the lender that can be paid directly to the loan officer, to the consumer, or a combination of the two.

Since all fees paid in a real estate transaction must be disclosed on the GFE, the YSP must be disclosed as well, but interestingly enough only mortgage brokers are required to disclose this charge, whereas direct lenders are not.

Historically, the mortgage broker, not knowing exactly what rate/ YSP offerings would be available when the loan is actually locked, would have to give a range. Over the years, brokers would disclose on the GFE, "Yield Spread Premium 0–3%."

This disclosure would tell the consumer that if there is a YSP it will be anywhere from zero to 3 percent. On a $300,000 loan that disclosure meant there may be a charge from no dollars to $9,000. That disclosure method really made no sense and didn't help the borrower make a decision when comparing one lender to a mortgage broker. It was meaningless information.

The new rules require the mortgage broker to disclose the exact amount of yield spread when the loan is locked. Brokers have for years thought this is unfair to them because bankers don't have to disclose the same information.

Either way, if a mortgage broker discloses a YSP amount for, say, a rate of 7.00 percent, then any other banker would also have a YSP coming to them as well.

You can start negotiating lender charges at any point during the comparison period where you're letting two or more lenders compete for your business, or you can begin your negotiations after you've selected your lender.

One important note here, once you select your lender, know that because of the new HVCC rules for appraisals, if you move your loan to another lender you'll have to pay for a new appraisal. So take care.

The first part of the lender fee negotiation begins with origination fees and discount points. Origination fees and points are a product of the interest rate you select. Recall how the more points you pay, the lower the rate you get? It's a tradeoff, really. For each point or origination fee you pay, you should lower your rate by a quarter percent. To reduce either the origination fee or the point you'll pay more. To save on closing costs, strongly consider not paying either, as the math rarely works out.

Don't forget the YSP. The YSP, the points, and the origination charges represent the bulk of the loan officers' commission, which she typically shares with her employer. Most loan officers get a 50/50 split with their employer when they close a loan. For example, on a $300,000 loan with a 1 percent origination fee and a YSP of 0.50, that adds up to 1.50 percent of $300,000, or $4,500. The loan officer splits that amount with the employer and makes $2,250.

When you negotiate the origination fee and points, remember that you're also negotiating what the loan officer will make from closing your loan. It's the loan officer's paycheck you're trying to dwindle down.

JUNK FEES

The second set of fees that can be open for negotiation are the junk fees. These are commonly named "processing" or "underwriting" or "administration" fees but can be called almost anything the lender or mortgage broker wants. The same is said for the "mortgage broker fee" which is simply their profit on the loan. These fees can come in two types: fees required to be collected and fees that are not required. Required fees aren't typically negotiable; they have to be paid. Lenders use loan processors to process loans, and a processing fee is set aside when the loan closes to pay the processor.

Other fees may or may not be required, but when loan officers agree to waive a processing fee, they do so at their own peril. If loan officers waive a required fee, the employer will take it all out of the loan officers' commissions. When loan officers refuse to waive a fee, it's because they might lose money on the loan or do a free one. For example:

Loan amount is $100,000 and there is a 1 percent mortgage broker fee, a 0.50 YSP, and a $500 processing fee. The processing fee is a required fee.

The total proceeds on this loan would be $2,000. Splitting that amount with the loan officer's employer would result in a $1,000 commission check. But if you try and have the loan officer waive the $500 processing fee, that $500 would be deducted entirely from the loan officers' paycheck, and she'd only make $500. That's not very much money for a loan officer to make on a loan, so if you experience a lot of resistance on having a lender or broker fee removed, it's because the loan officer can't afford to adhere to your request.

Lender or broker fees are where you can start negotiating your closing costs but there are a couple of other things you can do.

MONEY FOR THE DOWN PAYMENT AND CLOSING COSTS

You've determined how much you want for a down payment and figured out the lowest amount of closing costs you'll have to pay at closing, so the next thing to ask is, "Where do I get that money?"

If you've decided that you want a conventional loan with 20 percent down and that closing costs will add to the total, your funds to close requirement might be $30,000 and you only have $15,000. You've also decided not to take PMI and you don't want a piggyback with the higher rate. You're short $15,000. Let's go find some more money.

Adjust Your Rate: Let the Lender Pay Your Closing Costs

Recall that the higher your rate, the more YSP there is available. If you decide to increase your 30-year rate from 6.00 percent to 6.50

percent, there are about two points available. One would likely go to the lender and there's one left for you. That means the lender can credit you one point toward your closing costs.

On a $300,000 loan, you would get a $3,000 credit. The difference in payments?

6.00%	$1,798
6.50%	$1,896

Yes, the payments are about $100 higher with the higher rate, but you saved $3,000 in closing costs. Each time you consider different rates, compute the difference in monthly payments and then divide that savings into the closing costs. The result is the length of time it takes to recover those fees. In this example, it would be about 30 months, or 2.5 years.

When you see lender advertisements touting "No points! No closing costs!" this is what's happening. Rates are adjusted to cover the fees, and every lender and mortgage broker can accomplish the same thing.

Another way to save on closing costs is to have the seller pay for them. In fact, that's probably the simplest way to avoid or reduce your very own settlement charges. When you buy a house and write up a contract to make an offer, as part of your offer your agent will say something like, "We'll pay you $200,000 for this house as long as you pay $3,000 of my closing costs."

The seller can agree or disagree, but that's part of the negotiation process. This method doesn't work as well where real estate markets are considered a seller's market, meaning the local economy is doing well and home sales are brisk. Why would a seller give away $3,000 to a buyer when they can simply wait for the next offer?

However, sellers are more inclined to offer to pay for buyers' closing costs as an inducement to get an offer on their home. Their "For Sale" sign might read "Seller Pays Closing Costs" or something similar. Recall that sellers can't provide for down payments due to the new FHA rules but they can still pay buyers' closing costs.

One final note about closing costs: I get an occasional e-mail from someone asking if they can roll their closing costs into their loan, and the answer is usually no when it's a purchase and yes when it's a refinance.

There are a few exceptions with a purchase, and it involves government loans. VA loans have their funding fee of 2.15 percent, and that amount can be rolled into their loan. FHA loans have their mortgage insurance premium, or MIP. That can also be rolled into the loan amount, so long as the new amount doesn't exceed FHA loan limits for the area.

Gifts Are Little Known Sources for Down Payment and Closing Cost Money

We previously discussed gifts, who can give them and who cannot, but that is typically the first place to look for additional funds. One final point on gift funds is that they truly must be a gift and not a loan. A loan is something that must be paid back, and additional monthly payments could affect the ability to repay the mortgage. When a loan goes into default, the lender begins an investigation, and if there is a gift involved the lender could discover monthly payments for the gift that weren't previously disclosed. That's loan fraud, and the lender is likely to do more than just take the property back. Lenders can sue if they've been defrauded.

All loans that have gift funds will have an accompanying "gift affidavit" letter that is signed by the donor swearing that the funds are a gift and are not expected to be repaid. The lender will also want to verify that the donor has sufficient funds for the gift by reviewing the donors' bank statements and, finally, documenting the transfer from the donor to the buyer.

Note, the affidavit says the donor does not "expect" repayment. It doesn't bar someone from deciding later on to give the gift back when the home sells, for example. There are also potential income tax implications when receiving gifts, so be sure and check with a tax professional about the tax consequences and gifts.

You Can Use Retirement Account 401(k)s and IRAs

When I speak to homebuyers who are struggling to come up with money to close on a deal, if gift funds aren't an option I then ask if they have a 401(k) at work. Most do, and most 401(k) plans allow for a buyer to borrow money from the 401(k).

401(k) accounts have a vested balance, which the amount is entitled to the employee. 401(k) accounts typically allow an employee to borrow up to 50 percent of their vested balance. If, for instance, the vested balance is $10,000, then the employee may borrow $5,000. The 50 percent limit is there in case the employee leaves the company. The employee would need to immediately repay the loan upon termination, and if not, the remaining $5,000 left in the account would be applied to any outstanding loan.

Almost every 401(k) plan allows for the employee to borrow money in order to buy a home, while still other plans don't care what the money is used for. You'll need to check with your plan administrator to get the details on how your plan works.

Typical plans allow you to choose a term from one to five years, and the interest rates are perhaps the most competitive around. Each pay period, your employer would take out a portion of your earnings and apply it to your 401(k) loan.

First-time homebuyers may also take money out of their 401(k) as a loan in order to buy a house. These tax- and penalty-free withdrawals are usually limited to $10,000, but you'll need to check with your particular plan.

IRAs are also a source for down-payment funds, and first-time homebuyers can also tap into the IRA without penalty in order to buy real estate.

Borrowing from a 401(k) or withdrawing money from a 401(k) or

IRA can have tax and earning consequences. Once you withdraw money from the account, you stop earning interest on the amount withdrawn. Many financial planners will advise leaving a retirement account alone.

However, if you take money out of a retirement account and the stock market goes down or your fund begins to lose value, you'll actually benefit because you withdrew funds before a market down turn, shielding them from future losses. If you take money out of an IRA early and it's not to buy real estate, it is considered an early withdrawal and you will be penalized 10 percent of whatever you withdrew, plus pay income taxes on the withdrawn amount.

Those penalties don't apply if you replace those funds within 60 days of the withdrawal. I call this a *temporary withdrawal* because the withdrawal is short term. You can withdraw the funds from the IRA and then replace them later with other funds from other sources. This is only to be considered if you are certain you have replacement funds coming but you can't get to them quickly enough, such as the funds from the sale of an asset.

I used a 401(k) loan to buy my first house and it worked out wonderfully. A house came on the market sooner than I was really ready to buy and I only had enough for 10 percent down and closing costs, but I wanted to avoid PMI because it wasn't tax deductible then. I borrowed funds from my 401(k) balance to help close the deal and oddly, soon thereafter the markets started to take a dive for the next 18 months. Had I not borrowed from my 401(k), my balances would have actually dwindled due to market conditions. I was lucky, I know, but that's what happened.

You Can Use Appraisable Assets to Get Money for a Down Payment

Down payment and closing cost money can also be obtained by selling something. Lenders will always source your funds, meaning they want to know exactly where your down payment and closing cost funds are coming from. They want to make certain the funds belong to you and you haven't borrowed them from someone else who might want to be paid back. But you can raise money by selling certain items—but only items that have an appraisable value. Appraisable items mean anything that a third party can verify the approximate market value of. For instance, an automobile certainly has a market value that can be verified by a third party. I can look up the value of my Jeep online or get a book that lists current values of automobiles. But the key is the third-party appraisal.

If you have valuable artwork, say a sketch signed by Salvador Dali, you can take that artwork in to an art appraiser, who can assign a current value to the sketch. The third-party verification is important when appraising artwork.

I think I'm a pretty good artist and I could paint a picture of a beautiful sunset but I couldn't sell it to anyone. Nor could an art appraiser assign any value. There is no market for my paintings.

If you have an asset that can be sold, once you make the sale, take care in documenting the sale with a sales receipt of some kind and track the deposit in your account with an updated bank statement and deposit slip.

You don't have to sell the asset; you can also borrow against it. If you've got a box of old baseball cards you can get a value assigned to it by a baseball card appraiser. If you have someone willing to loan you some money, you can do that with the cards as the collateral.

You'll need to draw up the terms of your agreement, have both parties sign it, and count the monthly payments, if any, in your debt ratios. In this instance, loans secured by an appraisable asset need to have loan terms with at least a two-year minimum term to repay. Anything less than two years won't be acceptable to a mortgage lender.

Some Employers Assist with Mortgages

Many companies, large ones that can afford it, can also assist an employee with funds to buy a home, either as a grant or as a company loan—similar to how a 401(k) loan is structured. These programs used to be more popular than they are today, but it's worth a call to your human resource department.

Seller Carrybacks Might Be an Option

Sellers can help with your closing cost funds by acting as a lender and carrying a second mortgage. Second mortgages at banks are higher in rate than first mortgages are. If you can get a first mortgage rate at 6.00 percent, then a second mortgage might go for 7.50 percent.

Should your goal be to put 20 percent down to avoid PMI and you don't want a second mortgage due to the higher rates associated with them, then a seller could entertain carrying back a second mortgage.

If, for instance, you could have the seller carry back a second mortgage at 6.00 percent, then haven't you accomplished your initial goal of avoiding PMI and the higher rates associated with second mortgages?

You'll need to have your second mortgage drawn up so that it complies with lending laws in your state, and the loan will need to be for at least five years. The lender for the first mortgage will want to review the seller's note, and it will be included on your loan application.

Government Grants and Loans Often Go Unused

Perhaps the most underutilized and widely available source of funds to close is from your local and state governments.

Typically issued to first-timers, these programs act as outright grants that don't ever have to be paid back or payment-free loans that only have to be paid back if the home is sold within a certain period of time, most often seven years.

A homebuyer can apply for these funds directly with the agency sponsoring the program. The borrowers will need to prove they haven't owned a home in the previous three years and also show the loan approval from their lender. Typical grant and loan amounts can be as high as $10,000 or more and can be used for down payments, as well as for closing costs.

Some programs also have income limits in order to qualify for a grant or a loan, and often those limits are the median income for the area where they're buying. It's also possible that certain other restrictions can be placed on the funds, which the borrowers must follow. These vary by locale. A city could promote living downtown and require the property be located in a specific geographic area near downtown. Other grant and loan programs that aren't reserved for first-timers are available for public servants such as police and firefighters. Still other programs are set aside for teachers in public schools.

If you're looking for cash to close, use the search term "down payment assistance programs for *Your Town, Your State*," and you'll see a list of available funds.

SUMMARY

- ➤ Zero-down loans have been mostly eliminated.
- ➤ Some closing costs are negotiable but most are not.
- ➤ Nonlender charges are typically nonnegotiable.
- ➤ Reduced appraisal charges are available for well-qualified borrowers.
- ➤ GFEs must be resigned by borrowers before closing if the final fees are higher than originally disclosed to the borrower.
- ➤ A new consumer-friendly GFE has been introduced.
- ➤ The Fed acts to control the cost of money, not set your mortgage rate.
- ➤ Decide on the loan program you want before shopping; don't change your mind.

➤ Rate quotes are no good unless you lock in the rate with your lender.

➤ Increasing your rate increases the YSP and can be used to offset closing costs.

➤ Little-known sources of down payment and closing cost funds are available.

What to Do When Things Go Wrong

THE MORTGAGE DEBACLE in the 2000s changed the way lenders did things forever. It also changed the lives of people everywhere. Lenders are still licking their wounds for all the bad loans they made. In fact, most of the lenders who made all those subprime and alternative loans are out of business. But all too many buyers of those homes found themselves in serious trouble and are still recovering today. Many faced foreclosure right square in the face and won. Some lost.

As a lender makes a loan, the agreement is to get paid back on the first of the month, every month until the note is retired. If the note isn't paid by the fifteenth of the month, a late payment will be assessed, normally about 5 percent of the payment due.

So far, nothing has been reported to the credit bureaus other than you've made your payments on time with no payments being more than 30 days late. Then something goes wrong. You lose your job, or you get sick and can't work. Maybe someone in your family gets sick and you have to stay home to take care of the person.

Perhaps you have a hybrid mortgage or an ARM that is about to adjust so high that you'll no longer be able to make payments. Maybe you bought the property with intentions of selling it quickly for a profit without having to make a payment. What happens?

THE FORECLOSURE TIMELINE

After 30 days have passed and the lender still hasn't received payment, the late payment will be reported to the credit bureaus and your score will drop dramatically. After the forty-fifth day and a payment hasn't been received, your loan will be flagged at the mortgage company as possibly going into default. Your phone begins to ring from the mortgage company, but you're not sure what to tell them, so you don't answer.

So far, you've missed one payment. Day 60 goes by, and still no payment has been made. Your loan officially goes into the NOD state, or *notice of default*. The NOD is required to be sent to consumers notifying them that the lender intends to take back the property or expects to be paid the full amount within 30 days. If after 90 days no more payments have been made, the loan will go into foreclosure.

Different states have different foreclosure rules as to when a loan can actually be foreclosed on, but lenders across the nation follow these guidelines. Note that I said "guidelines" and not requirements.

In the early to mid-2000s, home prices were still on the rise. If a homeowner got behind on the mortgage, he could always sell the property and get out from under the debt. There are closing costs on a sale, just as there are costs when buying a home. The costs can be greater on a sale, primarily due to the commissions earned by real estate agents who list the home. Depending on where you live, agent commissions can be anywhere from 4 to 6 percent or more. There are discount agent services where the agent does little more than place your home on the multiple listing service, but most homes that are sold and marketed properly need a skilled agent.

There are also "for sale by owner" options, or FSBO (fizz-bow), which can save on agent commissions to keep the costs down as well—but again, if you need to sell, you need the experience and marketing techniques that agents can provide. Either way, there are additional costs on a sale not found on a purchase.

Lets take an example of how a sale might take place.

Sales price	$300,000
Closing costs	$20,000
Loan payoff	$100,000
Proceeds to seller	$180,000

Now the loan is paid off and the lender is satisfied. But what if the home doesn't have all that much equity?

Sales price	$300,000
Closing costs	$20,000
Loan payoff	$280,000
Proceeds to seller	−0−

The seller didn't walk away with any money, but the burden of the mortgage has disappeared. Now let's look at this one more time when the loan balance and closing costs exceed the sales price.

Sales price	$300,000
Closing costs	$20,000
Loan payoff	$300,000
Proceeds to seller	($20,000)

This means the seller has to come to the closing table writing a check instead of receiving one. The seller is "upside down" and would have to pay for the privilege of selling his home. But what if the seller couldn't come up with the $20,000? Or what if the sales price was even less than $300,000 and the seller had to come into the closing with still more funds? After all, if the seller had $20,000 or more in a bank account, he's likely not behind on his mortgage.

The owner needs to do something or he will lose the house completely and a foreclosure will appear on his credit report, meaning he won't be able to obtain another mortgage for four years.

SHORT SALES

A short sale is when a bank or lender agrees to accept a smaller amount of money to settle the mortgage account. A *short sale* isn't an automatic; lenders hate them. It eats up their assets and they have a house when they'd rather have the money, but sometimes the lender agrees to a short sale instead of foreclosing on a property.

When a home is listed for sale and it appears the sales price won't be enough to cover the closing costs and loan payoff, you'll need to begin the process of a short sale. This is difficult to do when working directly with the bank, and I strongly suggest you use an agent experienced in negotiating short sales because there will definitely be some negotiations between you and the lender. There's a lot to do to convince a lender to accept less than what is owed on the property. Before you contact the lender, you'll want to gather some documentation.

You'll Need Documentation to Get a Short Sale Approved

The first is your listing agreement, or even better, a listing agreement along with a purchase contract. There are agents who specialize in buying short sales, so they may have already done their research and have prepared an offer that is offering less than what is owed to the bank.

The listing agreement will show what the home is listed for on the multiple listing service. In addition to the listing agreement, the bank will want to see a comparative market analysis, or CMA, prepared by your agent, which will show what homes are selling for in your area. This is sort of a "mini" appraisal and looks at recent sales data that would support the current values.

Your agent should also provide the "net sheet" which is a tool agents use to show you how much (or how little) you would "net" from the sale of the home. The net sheet on a short sale would show you coming in with a considerable amount of money.

You'll also want to gather your current financials, such as your bank and retirement statements and your current income status showing copies of pay stubs from your employer.

Finally, you'll want to compose an explanation letter of why you need a short sale in the first place and be prepared to document your situation. This is your "hard luck" letter that would explain why you are where you are and what you are doing to alleviate the situation. Provide documentation of the loss of income, such as a letter from a previous employer or copies of any unemployment compensation you're receiving.

Different lenders will have different degrees and types of documentation requirements, but you can expect this list of documentation as a minimum.

Work Out Your Short Sale

Your next step is to contact the lender and track down the "workout" department. Your first contact will likely be with a customer service person who will begin the work on your short sale request, but ideally, you want to work further up the ladder to try and get the name of a supervisor in the workout department.

The workout department is aptly named because it tries to work things out with the borrower. In fact, people from the workout department were some of several people at the bank who were placing calls to you wondering why you hadn't paid your mortgage. Lenders need workouts as much as borrowers do.

The bank will likely ask for some money to perform a market

appraisal on your property in addition to doing its own research on the value of the property from its desk. The bank can do that by reviewing recent sales in your area.

If the bank finds that homes are selling for much more than what you're selling yours for, then it may not accept the short sale offer. You'll need to be prepared to respond if they say things like, "The home down the street sold for $100 per square foot and your short sale request is only $75 per square foot. Why is your offer so low?"

If a bank thinks it can get more money out of foreclosing on the property and then reselling it, a short sale might not be in your future. If, however, the bank sees that the short sale offer is reasonable and you're not making any money on the transaction, then your short sale request will likely be approved.

Negotiating a short sale can take time, especially if the bank is understaffed and the requests are many. That's why it's necessary to prepare your documentation ahead of time to facilitate the process.

One thing to note here: A short sale request doesn't have to be made when the borrower is behind on the mortgage. The borrower can be on time every time when the short sale request is made.

Your Request Might Get Turned Down: You Should Know Why

There are several reasons a request might be denied:

- ➤ *The seller doesn't qualify due to circumstances.* For instance the bank doesn't believe the story or the circumstances aren't dire enough to warrant accepting less on the property than what is owed.
- ➤ *The bank thinks the value is worth more than the listing price.* This might mean the bank thinks it would make more by foreclosing and selling the property than by accepting a short sale. There would have to be quite some disparity between the short sale request and the bank's estimated value, but it's still not an uncommon reason to decline the request.
- ➤ *The bank doesn't own the property any longer.* The bank might have

sold the loan to another lender or to Fannie or Freddie and doesn't have the authority to negotiate a short sale.

By addressing these issues beforehand and preparing for them, your short sale request is likely to be accepted rather than rejected.

Short Sales Affect Your Credit

After all, the initial loan terms you agreed to have essentially flown out the window. Do short sales affect your credit? The answer is yes, but it depends on the degree.

Most short sale requests are made by those who are in financial straits. There are current mortgage late payments appearing on the credit report and likely other credit accounts have been damaged as well.

In this instance, a short sale would have little, if any, effect on a credit score, because the real damage has already been done with previous last payments that are appearing.

If, however, there is no negative credit and the mortgage is current, it is up to the lender how it wants to report the short sale. You can make a request to the lender on how to report the short sale, but it's likely its policy has already been determined.

The credit report might read, "Paid as Agreed," or "Accepted Less Than What Is Owed," and a future lender reviewing the report could deem anything less than what was originally owed as a foreclosure. It's not an automatic, but if you ask ahead of time how it will be reported, you'll know in advance how your report will read. Different lenders may view short sales differently.

What If You're on the Buying Side of a Short Sale and Not the Seller?

First, have a little patience, and second, have your own financials in order. Short sales can take an agonizingly long time. I've seen short-sale negotiations take months, but if the property is researched thoroughly and all the financials are in order from both the seller and the buyer, then the process will be a smooth one.

What do buyers need? An ironclad approval from their lender of choice, and in a perfect world, an ironclad loan approval from the same lender who holds the current note on the property. You can get this information simply by asking the listing agent who the holder of the note is.

An ironclad approval means your approval documentation has been reviewed and approved by your lender—your pay stubs are in, your bank statements have been reviewed, and your AUS has been issued.

In fact, when you present yourself as an approved buyer, it can also help sway the current lender when considering a short sale.

What if your lender says no to a short sale or you don't want to sell but make every effort to keep the home? Then you want to look at a loan modification.

LOAN MODIFICATIONS

There are two types of loan modifications: One is for a rate and term change and the other is to modify the current note to make it more affordable.

A rate and term modification has been around for years and is simply a way for the borrower to contact the lender and request a lower interest rate instead of going through the entire refinance process and the associated costs. Now, however, loan modifications have taken center stage and are a key element of a bank's workout division.

A typical refinance requires the borrower to qualify all over again. If someone has a 7 percent rate and rates drop to 5 percent, the borrower would apply for a refinance loan, supply current pay stubs, and make sure the credit scores are above the minimum and the property has sufficient value in order to make the loan. But if the loan is suddenly unaffordable due to the ARM or hybrid resetting to a sky-high rate or the borrower has reduced income or there is no longer any equity in the property, then a regular refinance won't work.

A refinance loan will require a minimum of 10 percent equity in the deal. That would mean for a loan amount of $180,000, the property would need to appraise for at least $200,000.

Perhaps the debt ratios are above 50 and the borrower doesn't qualify because ratios are too high—or even worse, there have been some recent credit issues.

When you first contact the workout department at a bank asking for a loan modification, you'll encounter a customer service person who will see if you qualify for a workout arrangement over the phone. This arrangement will take any past-due balances and roll them into your loan amount and see if you still qualify from an income basis.

They will ask you how much money you make and go down a laundry list of items that you are currently obligated to pay, not including the mortgage. Car payments, child care, credit cards, even laundry and food expenses will be included.

If it is determined that your income is sufficient to meet your current obligations, then the lender will stop foreclosure proceedings and continue with your workout. This is most commonly used when a homeowner experiences a temporary reduction or elimination of income and thus fell on hard times but has recovered and wants to get caught up on payments but can't make all the payments at once. You will make a written application after the verbal interview is performed and provide bank statements and pay stubs and so on to complete the process.

If, however, there are some equity issues or your monthly debt load is too much to support the workout, then the loan can be taken to the next level.

If the monthly payment has adjusted so much the borrower can't afford the payments any longer, even though the income hasn't changed, then the lender can issue a loan modification. These new loan modification program must meet some criteria, but it's not as onerous as previous versions.

First, you must be able to qualify with current market rates. If your hybrid or ARM has reset to 10 percent and the new rates are at 6 percent, the lender will run your debt ratios using the 6 percent rate. If your rates are at or below 41 percent, then your loan is eligible for a modification.

You will still need to have a minimum of 10 percent of equity in the property as well if you're requesting a conventional modification; 3.5 percent equity if it's a qualifying FHA loan. VA loans aren't currently available for a VA to VA modification but can be modified with an FHA or conventional loan, given sufficient equity.

The real benefit of the new loan modification programs is allowing for a modification into an FHA loan, which requires less equity. It's not necessary to stay with a conventional modification. If the FHA loan limits support an FHA modification and your equity is relatively small, then explore the FHA modification program.

What the Home Affordable Refinance Program Means to You

The Home Affordable Refinance Program (HARP), introduced in 2009, addressed the biggest challenges facing homeowners who might go into foreclosure but haven't been able to modify using a traditional modification program due to equity or credit concerns. As long as the home loan is currently owned by Fannie or Freddie, the loan may be eligible. The HARP program doesn't ask for a minimum credit score but does require that the home not be in bankruptcy or foreclosure.

HARP addresses loans that are about to adjust into a higher rate

or that have equity problems and is applicable if the rate on the mortgage is being reduced or will be lower than what the new reset ARM
or hybrid rate will be. There is no minimum credit score on these
loans so people with less than a 620 score can still qualify. There's a
catch here, however; if the new payment is more than 20 percent
higher than the current payment, the minimum 620 score would
apply. HARP was designed to catch those who have seen their property values decline, since there is not enough equity in the property
for a refinance.

A HARP loan can go to 125 percent of the current appraised value
and still does not need mortgage insurance, even though the loan
amount would be more than 80 percent of the value of the home.
This means your loan amount to retire the old note could be
$105,000, while the appraisal would only come to $100,000. Under
traditional methods, a refinance or modification wouldn't work. Although the LTV can go up to 125 percent and still not need mortgage
insurance, the original loan must also not have had mortgage insurance, or the request won't be HARP eligible.

A HARP loan can't be a cash-out or equity loan but can only be
used to modify the rate and even the term. The term of the loan can
be changed as well, as long as the term is being reduced and not
lengthened.

Interestingly enough, it doesn't have to be for a primary residence. If the loan was originally issued as an investment and the
HARP request was also for an investment property (the occupancy of
the property didn't change), then the loan is still eligible for HARP.

The program also requires less documentation, as the assets and
income are *stated,* meaning the lender will use what is on the application. This part of the program sounds a little out of whack—after all,
wasn't it the "stated" thing that helped fuel the mortgage mess? But
if the rate is being reduced and the payments can be handled, then it
makes sense. The key here is to lower the payments and keep borrowers in their homes. In fact, government-backed refinances have had

the "stated" feature in their own refinance policy for decades and have been successful at it.

Remember, HARP is for Fannie- or Freddie-owned mortgages only. You might be sending your monthly payments to your lender who is servicing the loan, but it might have been sold to either Fannie or Freddie.

You can look to see if your loan is Fannie owned by visiting www.loanlookup.fanniemae.com, and for Freddie visit https://ww3 .freddiemac.com/corporate.

You Don't Need a Loan Modification Company

As expected, when loan modification gained popularity, then third-party loan modification companies began to pop up everywhere. These firms, for a fee, will take your application for you and negotiate directly with the lender on your behalf. Typically, these companies are legal firms, although they don't have to be.

I recall that when modification companies first gained popularity, I was besieged with e-mails from loan modification companies wanting to tell me, for a fee, how to become a loan modification expert.

Since loan officers are familiar with the loan process, it makes sense for loan officers to act as loan modification experts. On a side note, I find this notion interesting, as I place lots of blame for the past mortgage mess squarely on the shoulders of loan officers putting consumers in loans they never should have had in the first place.

I've seen loan modification pitches in e-mails, on postcards, and even door-to-door. It's a lead generation system, in most cases. The loan modification company hires people to send postcards or letters or e-mails to people who have received an NOD from their lender.

This notice of default is a public record and indicates that the homeowner is having trouble making payments to the lender and might be a candidate for a loan modification.

Sure, they might very well be. But a loan modification request doesn't have to be made by a loan modification company; it can be made by the homeowners if they so choose.

It is also true that the loan modification company runs through hundreds of modification requests and knows how to structure them properly—allegedly, that is.

The problem I have with loan modification companies is that they typically require a couple thousand dollars up front, with no guarantee the loan will be modified as presented. I also have a problem with loan modification companies when it comes to their competency.

If some people couldn't make it as (honest) loan officers, then what business do they have working with a loan modification firm? Little, if any, in my opinion.

There are legitimate loan modification companies, I'm sure, but it is hard to tell ahead of time, and it would also be hard to shell out a couple of thousand dollars to someone you've never heard of before.

After all, upfront fees are income to these folks with no guarantee to perform. You can fill out some paperwork, send in your $2,000, and then hear, "I'm sorry, your lender denied your request."

You could have done the same thing yourself by calling your lender for a workout, a conventional modification, or HARP loan.

Lenders do not, repeat, *do not* want to own real estate. It hurts their profitability and can put them out of business. They do everything they can to avoid foreclosing, but oftentimes, the lender has little choice but to move forward.

Want to know one of the biggest complaints I've heard from lenders regarding foreclosures? They never hear from the borrowers. They place calls and write letters with no response, and the homeowners don't think there's anything they can do, so they just pray and hope something good happens soon.

Lenders, however, don't know if the homeowner wants to keep

the property, and if there's no communication, the lender will finally assume there's nothing more it can do.

Lenders pay lots of people money to help their homeowners keep their homes. If you're someone or you know someone who is struggling, take it from me that picking up the phone and working something out with the lender is the best practice.

Lenders won't always agree to a workout or the modification won't work. It's not 100 percent. But what is 100 percent guaranteed is that the home will eventually be foreclosed on if the homeowner does nothing.

REPAIRING YOUR CREDIT

When homeowners find themselves in difficult situations financially, at some point their credit scores are going to be affected. Since certain minimum credit scores are now required, people who are behind on their mortgage need to do whatever it takes to keep their home, because qualifying for a new mortgage or even finding a place to rent will be difficult due to the damaged credit. So what to do when credit is damaged? Perhaps the best thing to do is simply wait for the credit to repair itself.

When people get themselves in credit trouble, they suddenly notice advertisements for "credit repair." It's not that they've suddenly appeared. They've always been there, it's just now that they're being noticed.

Credit repair companies allege they can legally repair your credit and charge you a fee for doing so. Although that may be so, they can only do what you yourself can do and not pay the fee.

Some advise that by placing a consumer letter in your credit report file explaining your situation, your credit will improve. The fact is that lenders rarely "read" a credit report, and instead look at your credit score. You may have written a heart-wrenching letter explaining your situation, but the potential lender will never read it. There is no reason to write an explanation letter to keep on file at the credit bureaus.

Others will, for a fee, attempt to dispute any negative items on your report. Consumer laws require that any disputed item on a credit report must be verified within 30 days or the bureaus must remove the negative items.

This is old school in a new world. If your credit report shows a late payment on your car from a couple of months ago and its valid, there's not a lot you can do about it other than call up the creditor and ask it to remove the item. The creditor will likely say no, but at least you tried.

What won't work is continually disputing the same item, hoping the creditor will fall asleep during the 30-day period and the negative information would then be removed.

Since credit scores are reviewed and not the literal reading of a late payment, even if a negative item were removed, the scores wouldn't change. Credit scores reflect recent activity on a credit report, and unless the credit-reporting agency is specifically asked to "rerun" a credit score without the negative information, the score won't change.

This is called a "rapid rescore" and is a legitimate method of getting scores up when incorrect information is showing up on a report. I recall a client who needed a minimum 700 score for a second mortgage and her score was 693. It was a 693 because it showed a recent credit card payment being made more than 30 days late.

She got the creditor to document the mistake, providing me with a letter on the creditor's letterhead. I forwarded that letter to the credit bureau asking for a rapid rescore. For about $30, a credit-reporting agency will take the corrected information and then calculate the new credit score as if the negative information were never there.

We did correct the report, her score then jumped to 740, and we got her loan approved.

Credit repair agencies may have had more impact several years ago when things were less automated, but these days it's nearly impossible to get information that is true and correct removed from a credit report.

What credit repair agencies can do, however, is put you on a path to fix your credit over an extended period of time. But, again, you can do this on your own. If you're currently experiencing negative credit but you can see your way out of it, here's how to fix it.

First, stop making late payments. That sounds simple enough, but by putting the bad stuff further and further in the rear view mirror, your score will improve. Because credit scores place the most weight on the most recent two-year period, negative information will soon be in the distant past. That doesn't mean after 7 or 10 years—getting the bad information on your report as soon as 24 months ago means your scores will begin to rise, as long as you continue making timely payments.

At the same time, make sure you pay your balances down to the magical 30 percent level. If your credit limits are $10,000, then by keeping a $3,000 regular balance, your scores will also begin to improve. If your collection accounts or judgments are simply too many to manage, then perhaps it is time to visit a bankruptcy attorney.

If your situation is a temporary one, meaning whatever went wrong is now fixed, then simply do the things you used to do that got you good credit in the first place and wait—you'll soon find your scores are where they need to be, and you didn't have to pay anyone for the privilege.

SUMMARY

- ➢ Foreclosures follow a strict timeline, yet states can control certain dates.
- ➢ If property is worth less than what is owed, consider a short sale.

- Successful short-sale negotiations require some homework up front.
- Short sales will affect credit reports negatively, but it is up to the lender to decide how to report it.
- Ask for a loan modification if you don't want to sell.
- Don't pay third parties to negotiate a loan modification.
- The HARP program was introduced to help people refinance out of their bad mortgage into a lower fixed-rate payment.
- Repair your credit on your own.

Monthly Payment Schedules

THE FOLLOWING SCHEDULE shows monthly payments per thousand dollars financed. To calculate your monthly payment:

1. Find your interest rate in the first column.
2. Move across to the appropriate column for your term.
3. Multiply that number by the number of thousand dollars financed.

EXAMPLE

If you are borrowing $150,000 at 6.50 percent interest for a 30-year term:

$6.32 × 150 (thousands) = $948.00 principal and interest payment

Thus, your monthly payment for both principal and interest is $948.

Rate	40 years	30 years	25 years	20 years	15 years	10 years
2.500	$3.30	$3.95	$4.49	$5.30	$6.67	$9.43
2.625	$3.37	$4.02	$4.55	$5.36	$6.73	$9.48
2.750	$3.44	$4.08	$4.61	$5.42	$6.79	$9.54
2.875	$3.51	$4.15	$4.68	$5.48	$6.85	$9.60
3.000	$3.58	$4.22	$4.74	$5.55	$6.91	$9.66
3.125	$3.65	$4.28	$4.81	$5.61	$6.97	$9.71
3.250	$3.73	$4.35	$4.87	$5.67	$7.03	$9.77
3.375	$3.80	$4.42	$4.94	$5.74	$7.09	$9.83
3.500	$3.87	$4.49	$5.01	$5.80	$7.15	$9.89
3.625	$3.95	$4.56	$5.07	$5.86	$7.21	$9.95
3.750	$4.03	$4.63	$5.14	$5.93	$7.27	$10.01
3.875	$4.10	$4.70	$5.21	$5.99	$7.33	$10.07
4.000	$4.18	$4.77	$5.28	$6.06	$7.40	$10.12
4.125	$4.26	$4.85	$5.35	$6.13	$7.46	$10.18
4.250	$4.34	$4.92	$5.42	$6.19	$7.52	$10.24
4.375	$4.42	$4.99	$5.49	$6.26	$7.59	$10.30
4.500	$4.50	$5.07	$5.56	$6.33	$7.65	$10.36
4.625	$4.58	$5.14	$5.63	$6.39	$7.71	$10.42
4.750	$4.66	$5.22	$5.70	$6.46	$7.78	$10.48
4.875	$4.74	$5.29	$5.77	$6.53	$7.84	$10.55
5.000	$4.82	$5.37	$5.85	$6.60	$7.91	$10.61
5.125	$4.91	$5.44	$5.92	$6.67	$7.97	$10.67
5.250	$4.99	$5.52	$5.99	$6.74	$8.04	$10.73
5.375	$5.07	$5.60	$6.07	$6.81	$8.10	$10.79
5.500	$5.16	$5.68	$6.14	$6.88	$8.17	$10.85
5.625	$5.24	$5.76	$6.22	$6.95	$8.24	$10.91
5.750	$5.33	$5.84	$6.29	$7.02	$8.30	$10.98
5.875	$5.42	$5.92	$6.37	$7.09	$8.37	$11.04
6.000	$5.50	$6.00	$6.44	$7.16	$8.44	$11.10

Rate	40 years	30 years	25 years	20 years	15 years	10 years
6.125	$5.59	$6.08	$6.52	$7.24	$8.51	$11.16
6.250	$5.68	$6.16	$6.60	$7.31	$8.57	$11.23
6.375	$5.77	$6.24	$6.67	$7.38	$8.64	$11.29
6.500	$5.85	$6.32	$6.75	$7.46	$8.71	$11.35
6.625	$5.94	$6.40	$6.83	$7.53	$8.78	$11.42
6.750	$6.03	$6.49	$6.91	$7.60	$8.85	$11.48
6.875	$6.12	$6.57	$6.99	$7.68	$8.92	$11.55
7.000	$6.21	$6.65	$7.07	$7.75	$8.99	$11.61
7.125	$6.31	$6.74	$7.15	$7.83	$9.06	$11.68
7.250	$6.40	$6.82	$7.23	$7.90	$9.13	$11.74
7.375	$6.49	$6.91	$7.31	$7.98	$9.20	$11.81
7.500	$6.58	$6.99	$7.39	$8.06	$9.27	$11.87
7.625	$6.67	$7.08	$7.47	$8.13	$9.34	$11.94
7.750	$6.77	$7.16	$7.55	$8.21	$9.41	$12.00
7.875	$6.86	$7.25	$7.64	$8.29	$9.48	$12.07
8.000	$6.95	$7.34	$7.72	$8.36	$9.56	$12.13
8.125	$7.05	$7.42	$7.80	$8.44	$9.63	$12.20
8.250	$7.14	$7.51	$7.88	$8.52	$9.70	$12.27
8.375	$7.24	$7.60	$7.97	$8.60	$9.77	$12.33
8.500	$7.33	$7.69	$8.05	$8.68	$9.85	$12.40
8.625	$7.43	$7.78	$8.14	$8.76	$9.92	$12.47
8.750	$7.52	$7.87	$8.22	$8.84	$9.99	$12.53
8.875	$7.62	$7.96	$8.31	$8.92	$10.07	$12.60
9.000	$7.71	$8.05	$8.39	$9.00	$10.14	$12.67
9.125	$7.81	$8.14	$8.48	$9.08	$10.22	$12.74
9.250	$7.91	$8.23	$8.56	$9.16	$10.29	$12.80
9.375	$8.00	$8.32	$8.65	$9.24	$10.37	$12.87
9.500	$8.10	$8.41	$8.74	$9.32	$10.44	$12.94
9.625	$8.20	$8.50	$8.82	$9.40	$10.52	$13.01

Rate	40 years	30 years	25 years	20 years	15 years	10 years
9.750	$8.30	$8.59	$8.91	$9.49	$10.59	$13.08
9.875	$8.39	$8.68	$9.00	$9.57	$10.67	$13.15
10.000	$8.49	$8.78	$9.09	$9.65	$10.75	$13.22
10.125	$8.59	$8.87	$9.18	$9.73	$10.82	$13.28
10.250	$8.69	$8.96	$9.26	$9.82	$10.90	$13.35
10.375	$8.79	$9.05	$9.35	$9.90	$10.98	$13.42
10.500	$8.89	$9.15	$9.44	$9.98	$11.05	$13.49
10.625	$8.98	$9.24	$9.53	$10.07	$11.13	$13.56
10.750	$9.08	$9.33	$9.62	$10.15	$11.21	$13.63
10.875	$9.18	$9.43	$9.71	$10.24	$11.29	$13.70
11.000	$9.28	$9.52	$9.80	$10.32	$11.37	$13.78
11.125	$9.38	$9.62	$9.89	$10.41	$11.44	$13.85
11.250	$9.48	$9.71	$9.98	$10.49	$11.52	$13.92
11.375	$9.58	$9.81	$10.07	$10.58	$11.60	$13.99
11.500	$9.68	$9.90	$10.16	$10.66	$11.68	$14.06
11.625	$9.78	$10.00	$10.26	$10.75	$11.76	$14.13
11.750	$9.88	$10.09	$10.35	$10.84	$11.84	$14.20
11.875	$9.98	$10.19	$10.44	$10.92	$11.92	$14.27
12.000	$10.08	$10.29	$10.53	$11.01	$12.00	$14.35
12.125	$10.19	$10.38	$10.62	$11.10	$12.08	$14.42
12.250	$10.29	$10.48	$10.72	$11.19	$12.16	$14.49
12.375	$10.39	$10.58	$10.81	$11.27	$12.24	$14.56
12.500	$10.49	$10.67	$10.90	$11.36	$12.33	$14.64
12.625	$10.59	$10.77	$11.00	$11.45	$12.41	$14.71
12.750	$10.69	$10.87	$11.09	$11.54	$12.49	$14.78
12.875	$10.79	$10.96	$11.18	$11.63	$12.57	$14.86
13.000	$10.90	$11.06	$11.28	$11.72	$12.65	$14.93
13.125	$11.00	$11.16	$11.37	$11.80	$12.73	$15.00
13.250	$11.10	$11.26	$11.47	$11.89	$12.82	$15.08

Rate	40 years	30 years	25 years	20 years	15 years	10 years
13.375	$11.20	$11.36	$11.56	$11.98	$12.90	$15.15
13.500	$11.30	$11.45	$11.66	$12.07	$12.98	$15.23
13.625	$11.40	$11.55	$11.75	$12.16	$13.07	$15.30
13.750	$11.51	$11.65	$11.85	$12.25	$13.15	$15.38
13.875	$11.61	$11.75	$11.94	$12.34	$13.23	$15.45
14.000	$11.71	$11.85	$12.04	$12.44	$13.32	$15.53
14.125	$11.81	$11.95	$12.13	$12.53	$13.40	$15.60
14.250	$11.92	$12.05	$12.23	$12.62	$13.49	$15.68
14.375	$12.02	$12.15	$12.33	$12.71	$13.57	$15.75
14.500	$12.12	$12.25	$12.42	$12.80	$13.66	$15.83
14.625	$12.22	$12.35	$12.52	$12.89	$13.74	$15.90
14.750	$12.33	$12.44	$12.61	$12.98	$13.83	$15.98
14.875	$12.43	$12.54	$12.71	$13.08	$13.91	$16.06
15.000	$12.53	$12.64	$12.81	$13.17	$14.00	$16.13
15.125	$12.64	$12.74	$12.91	$13.26	$14.08	$16.21
15.250	$12.74	$12.84	$13.00	$13.35	$14.17	$16.29
15.375	$12.84	$12.94	$13.10	$13.45	$14.25	$16.36
15.500	$12.94	$13.05	$13.20	$13.54	$14.34	$16.44
15.625	$13.05	$13.15	$13.30	$13.63	$14.43	$16.52
15.750	$13.15	$13.25	$13.39	$13.73	$14.51	$16.60
15.875	$13.25	$13.35	$13.49	$13.82	$14.60	$16.67
16.000	$13.36	$13.45	$13.59	$13.91	$14.69	$16.75
16.125	$13.46	$13.55	$13.69	$14.01	$14.77	$16.83
16.250	$13.56	$13.65	$13.79	$14.10	$14.86	$16.91
16.375	$13.67	$13.75	$13.88	$14.19	$14.95	$16.99
16.500	$13.77	$13.85	$13.98	$14.29	$15.04	$17.06
16.625	$13.87	$13.95	$14.08	$14.38	$15.13	$17.14
16.750	$13.98	$14.05	$14.18	$14.48	$15.21	$17.22
16.875	$14.08	$14.16	$14.28	$14.57	$15.30	$17.30

Rate	40 years	30 years	25 years	20 years	15 years	10 years
17.000	$14.18	$14.26	$14.38	$14.67	$15.39	$17.38
17.125	$14.29	$14.36	$14.48	$14.76	$15.48	$17.46
17.250	$14.39	$14.46	$14.58	$14.86	$15.57	$17.54
17.375	$14.49	$14.56	$14.68	$14.95	$15.66	$17.62
17.500	$14.60	$14.66	$14.78	$15.05	$15.75	$17.70
17.625	$14.70	$14.77	$14.87	$15.15	$15.84	$17.78
17.750	$14.80	$14.87	$14.97	$15.24	$15.92	$17.86
17.875	$14.91	$14.97	$15.07	$15.34	$16.01	$17.94
18.000	$15.01	$15.07	$15.17	$15.43	$16.10	$18.02

Glossary

Abstract of title A written record of the historical ownership of the property that helps to determine whether the property can, in fact, be transferred from one party to another without any previous claims. An abstract of title is used in certain parts of the country when determining if there are any previous claims on the subject property in question.

Acceleration A loan accelerates when it is paid off early, usually at the request or demand of the lender. An acceleration clause within a loan document states what must happen when a loan must be paid immediately; but usually it applies to nonpayment, late payments, or the transfer of the property without the lender's permission.

Adjustable rate mortgage A loan program where the interest rate may change throughout the life of the loan. An ARM adjusts based on terms agreed to between the lender and the borrower, but typically it may only change once or twice a year.

Alternative credit Items you must pay each month but that won't appear on your credit report, such as your telephone bill. In relation to mortgage loans, while such items aren't reported as installment or revolving credit, they can establish your ability and willingness to make consistent payments in a responsible manner. Sometimes called *nonstandard credit*.

Alt loans Alternative loans, so-called because they're not conventional or government loans but step outside the lending box and establish their own lending criteria.

Amortization Amortization is the length of time it takes for a loan to be fully paid off, by predetermined agreement. These payments are at regular intervals. Sometimes called a *fully amortized* loan. Amortization terms can vary, but generally accepted terms run in five-year increments, from 10 to 40 years.

Annual percentage rate The cost of money borrowed, expressed as an annual rate. The APR is a useful consumer tool to compare different lenders, but unfortunately, it is often not used correctly. The APR can only work when comparing the same exact loan type from one lender to another.

Appraisable asset Any item whose value can be determined by a third-party expert. That car you want to sell is an appraisable asset. If the item can be appraised, then you can use those funds to buy a house.

Appraisal A report that helps to determine the market value of a property. An appraisal can be done in various ways, as required by a lender, from simply driving by the property to ordering a full-blown inspection, complete with full-color photographs. Appraisals compare similar homes in the area to substantiate the value of the property in question.

APR See annual percentage rate.

ARM See adjustable rate mortgage.

Assumable mortgage Homes sold with assumable mortgages let buyers take over the terms of the loan, along with the house being sold. Assumable loans may be fully or nonqualifying assumable, meaning buyers take over the loan without being qualified or otherwise evaluated by the original lender. Qualifying assumable loans mean that while buyers may assume terms of the existing note, they must qualify all over again as if they were applying for a brand-new loan.

AUS See automated underwriting system.

Automated underwriting system A software application that electronically issues a preliminary loan approval. An AUS uses a complex approval matrix that reviews credit reports, debt ratios, and other factors that go into a mortgage loan approval.

Automated valuation model An electronic method of evaluating a property's appraised value, done by scanning public records for recent home sales and other data in the subject property's neighborhood. Although not yet widely accepted as a replacement for full-blown appraisals, many in the industry expect AVMs to eventually replace traditional appraisals altogether.

AVM *See* automated valuation model.

Balloon mortgage A type of mortgage where the remaining balance must be paid in full at the end of a preset term. A five-year balloon mortgage might be amortized over a 30-year period, but the remaining balance is due, in full, at the end of five years.

Basis point A basis point is 1/100 percent change in rate. A move of 50 basis points would cause a 30-year fixed mortgage rate to change by 1/8 percent.

Bridge loan A short-term loan primarily used to pull equity out of one property for a down payment on another. This loan is paid off when the original property sells. Since they are short-term loans, sometimes lasting just a few weeks, usually only retail banks offer them. Usually the borrower doesn't make any monthly payments and only pays off the loan when the property sells.

Bundling Bundling is the act of putting together several real estate or mortgage services in one package. Instead of paying for an appraisal here or an inspection there, some or all of the buyer's services are packaged together. Usually a bundle offers discounts on all services, although when they're bundled, it's hard to parse all the services to see whether you're getting a good deal.

Buydown Paying more money to get a lower interest rates is called a *permanent* buydown, and it is used in conjunction with discount points. The more points, the lower the rate. A *temporary* buydown is a fixed-rate mortgage that starts at a reduced rate for the first period, and then gradually increases to its final note rate. A temporary buydown for two years is called a 2–1 buydown. For three years, it is called a 3–2–1 buydown.

Cash-out A refinance mortgage that involves taking equity out of a home in the form of cash during a refinance. Instead of just reducing your interest rate during a refinance and financing your closing costs, you finance even more, putting the additional money in your pocket.

Closer The person who helps prepare the lender's closing documents. The closer forwards those documents to your settlement agent's office, where you will be signing closing papers. In some states, a closer can be the person who holds your loan closing.

Closing costs The various fees involved when buying a home or obtaining a mortgage. The fees, required to issue a good loan, can come directly from the lender or may come from others in the transactions.

Collateral Collateral is property owned by the borrower that's pledged to the lender as security in case the loan goes bad. A lender makes a mortgage with the house as collateral.

Comparable sales Comparable sales are that part of an appraisal report that lists recent transfers of similar properties in the immediate vicinity of the house being bought. Also called *comps.*

Conforming loan A conventional conforming loan is a Fannie Mae or Freddie Mac loan that is equal to or less than the maximum allowable loan limits established by Fannie and Freddie. These limits are changed annually.

Conventional loan A loan mortgage that uses guidelines established by Fannie Mae or Freddie Mac and is issued and guaranteed by lenders.

Correspondent banker A mortgage banker that doesn't intend to keep your mortgage loan, but instead sells your loan to another preselected mortgage banker. Correspondent bankers are smaller mortgage bankers, those perhaps with a regional presence but not a national one. They can shop various rates from other correspondent mortgage bankers that have set up an established relationship to buy and sell loans from one another. They operate much like a broker, except correspondent bankers use their own money to fund loans.

Credit report A report that shows the payment histories of a consumer, along with the individual's property addresses and any public records.

Credit repository A place where credit histories are stored. Merchants and banks agree to store consumers' credit patterns in a central place that other merchants and banks can access.

Credit score A number derived from a consumer's credit history and based on various credit details in a consumer's past and on the likelihood of default. Different credit patterns are assigned different numbers, and different credit activity may have a greater or lesser impact on the score. The higher the credit score, the better the credit.

Debt consolidation Paying off all or part of one's consumer debt with equity from a home. Debit consolidation can be part of a refinanced mortgage or a separate equity loan.

Debt ratio Gross monthly payments divided by gross monthly income, expressed as a percentage. There are typically two debt ratios to be considered: The *housing ratio*—sometimes called the front-end or front ratio—is the total monthly house payment, plus any monthly tax, insurance, private mortgage insurance, or homeowners association dues, divided by gross monthly income. The *total debt ratio*—also called the back-end or back ratio—is the total housing payment plus other monthly consumer installment or revolving debt, also expressed as a percentage. Loan debt ratio guidelines are usually denoted as 32/38, with 32 being the front ratio and 38 being the back ratio. Ratio guidelines can vary from loan to loan and lender to lender.

Deed A written document evidencing each transfer of ownership in a property.

Deed of trust A written document giving an interest in the home being bought to a third party, usually the lender, as security to the lender.

Delinquent Being behind on a mortgage payment. Delinquencies typically begin to be recognized as 30+ days delinquent, 60+ days delinquent, and 90+ days delinquent.

Discount points Also called *points,* they are represented as a percentage of a loan amount. One point equals 1 percent of a loan balance. Borrowers pay discount points to reduce the interest rate for a mortgage. Typically, each discount point paid reduces the interest rate by .025 percent. It is a form of prepaid interest to a lender.

Document stamp Evidence—usually with an ink stamp—of how much tax was paid upon transfer of ownership of property. Certain states call it a *doc stamp.* Doc stamp tax rates can vary based on locale, and not all states have doc stamps.

Down payment The amount of money initially given by the borrower to close a mortgage. The down payment equals the sales price less financing. It's the very first bit of equity you'll have in the new home.

Easement A right of way previously established by a third party. Easement types can vary but typically involve the right of a public utility to cross your land to access an electrical line.

Entitlement The amount the VA will guarantee in order for a VA loan to be made. *See also* VA loan.

Equity The difference between the appraised value of a home and any outstanding loans recorded against the house.

Escrow Depending on where you live, escrow can mean two things. On the West Coast, for example, when a home goes under contract, it "goes into escrow" (*see also* escrow agent). In other parts of the country, an escrow is a financial account set up by a lender to collect monthly installments for annual tax bills and/or hazard insurance policy renewals.

Escrow account See impound account.

Escrow agent On the West Coast, the escrow agent is the person or company that handles the home closing, ensuring documents are assigned correctly and property transfer has legitimately changed hands.

FACTA See Fair and Accurate Credit Transactions Act.

Fair and Accurate Credit Transactions Act The FACTA is a new law that replaces the Fair Credit Reporting Act, or FCRA, and governs how consumer information can be stored, shared, and monitored for privacy and accuracy.

Fair Credit Reporting Act The FCRA was the first consumer law that emphasized consumer rights and protections relating to consumers' credit reports, their credit applications, and privacy concerns.

Fannie Mae See Federal National Mortgage Association.

Farmers Home Administration The FmHA provides financing to farmers and other qualified borrowers who are unable to obtain loans elsewhere. These loans are typical for rural properties that might be larger in acreage than a suburban home, as well as for working farms.

FCRA *See* Fair Credit Reporting Act.

Fed Shorthand name for the Federal Reserve Board.

Federal Home Loan Mortgage Corporation The FHLMC, or Freddie Mac, is a corporation established by the U.S. government in 1968 to buy mortgages from lenders made under Freddie Mac guidelines.

Federal Housing Administration The FHA was formed in 1934 and is now a division of the Department of Housing and Urban Development (HUD). It provides loan guarantees to lenders who make loans under FHA guidelines.

Federal National Mortgage Association The FNMA, or Fannie Mae, was originally established in 1938 by the U.S. government to buy FHA mortgages and provide liquidity in the mortgage marketplace. It is similar in function to Freddie Mac. In 1968, its charter was changed and it now purchases conventional mortgages as well as government ones.

Federal Reserve Board The head of the Federal Reverse Banks that, among other things, sets overnight lending rates for banking institutions. The Fed does not set mortgage rates.

Fed funds rate The rate banks charge one another to borrow money overnight.

Fee income The closing costs received by a lender or broker that are outside of the interest rate or discount points. Fee income can be in the form of loan processing charges, underwriting fees, and the like.

FHA *See* Federal Housing Administration.

FICO FICO stands for Fair Isaac Corporation, the company that invented the most widely used credit scoring system.

Final inspection The last inspection of a property, showing that a new home being built is 100 percent complete or that a home improvement is 100 percent complete. It lets lenders know that their collateral and their loan are exactly where they should be.

Financed premium An alternative to second mortgages and mortgage insurance that allows for the borrower to buy a mortgage insurance premium and roll the cost of the premium into the loan amount, in lieu of paying a mortgage insurance payment every month.

Fixed rate mortgage A loan whose interest rate does not change throughout the term of the loan.

Float Actively deciding not to "lock" or guarantee an interest rate while a loan is being processed. A float is usually done because the borrower believes rates will go down.

Float-down A mortgage loan rate that can drop as mortgage rates drop. Usually a loan comes in two types of float, one being during construction of a home and the other being during the period of an interest rate lock.

Flood certificate A certificate that shows whether a property or part of a property lies above or below any local flood zones. These flood zones are mapped over the course of several years by the Federal Emergency Management Agency (FEMA). The certificate identifies the property's exact legal location and a flood line's elevation. There is a box that simply asks, "Is the property in a flood zone, yes or no?" If the property is in a flood zone, the lender will require special flood insurance that is not usually carried under a standard homeowners hazard insurance policy.

FmHA *See* Farmers Home Administration.

Foreclosure A foreclosure is the bad thing that happens when the mortgage isn't repaid. Lenders begin the process of forcefully recovering their collateral when borrowers fail to make loan payments. The lender takes your house away.

Freddie Mac *See* Federal Home Loan Mortgage Corporation.

Fully indexed rate The number reached when adding a loan's index and the margin. This rate is how adjustable note rates are compiled.

Funding The actual transfer of money from a lender to a borrower.

Funding fee A required fee, equal to 2 percent of the sales price of a home, that helps to fund a VA loan guarantee.

GFE *See* Good faith estimate.

Gift When the down payment and closing costs for a home are given to the borrower instead of the funds coming from their own accounts, it is called a gift. Usually such gifts can only come from family members or foundations established to help new homeowners.

Gift affidavit A form signed whereby someone swears that the money they're giving you is indeed a gift, not a loan, and is to be used for the purchase of a home. Lenders like to see that form, as well as a paper trail of the gift funds being added to your own funds.

Gift funds Monies given to a borrower for the sole purpose of buying a home. These funds are not to be paid back in any form and are usually given by a family member or a qualified nonprofit organization.

Ginnie Mae See Government National Mortgage Association.

Good faith estimate The GFE is list of estimated closing costs on a particular mortgage transaction. This estimate must be provided to the loan applicants within 72 hours after receipt of a mortgage application by the lender or broker.

Government National Mortgage Association The GNMA, or Ginnie Mae, is a U.S. government corporation formed to purchase government loans such as VA and FHA loans from banks and mortgage lenders. Think of it as Fannie or Freddie, only it buys government loans.

Hazard insurance A specific type of insurance that covers against certain destructive elements such as fire, wind, and hail. It is usually an addition to homeowners insurance, but every home loan has a hazard rider.

HELOC See Home Equity Line of Credit.

Hold-back A contingency fund associated with a construction or remodel. It covers any change orders that might occur during the process. A change order is what happens when you simply change your mind. The hold-back helps pay for the change when changing your mind costs more than the loan. A typical hold-back amount is 10 percent of the original loan.

Home Equity Line of Credit HELOC is a credit line using a home as collateral. Customers write checks on this line of credit whenever they need to and pay only on balances withdrawn. It is much like a credit card, but secured by the property.

Homeowners insurance An insurance policy that covers not just hazard items, but also other things, such as liability or personal property.

Hybrid loan A cross between an ARM and a fixed-rate loan. In a hybrid loan, the rate is fixed for a predetermined number of years before turning into an adjustable rate mortgage, or ARM.

Impound account An account that is set up by a lender to deposit a monthly portion of annual property taxes or hazard insurance. As taxes or insurance come up for renewal, the lender pays the bill using these funds. Also called an *escrow account.*

Index An index is used as the basis to establish an interest rate, usually associated with a margin. Most anything can be an index, but the most common are U.S. treasuries or similar instruments. *See also* fully indexed rate.

Inspection A structural review of the house to determine defects in workmanship, damage to the property, or required maintenance. An inspection does not determine value of the property. A pest inspection, for example, looks for termites or wood ants.

Installment account Borrowing one lump sum and agreeing to pay back a certain amount each month until the loan is paid off. A car loan is an example of an installment loan.

Intangible asset An asset not by itself, but by what it represents. A publicly traded stock is an intangible asset. It's not the stock itself that has the value, but what the stock represents in terms of income.

Intangible tax A state tax on personal property.

Interest-only loan A loan that requires only that you pay the interest on your loan each month, without having to pay any part of the principal.

Interest rate The amount charged to borrowed money over a specified period of time.

Interest rate reduction loan An IRRL is a VA refinance loan program that has relaxed credit guidelines. Also called a streamline refinance.

IRRL *See* interest rate reduction loan.

Jumbo loan A mortgage that exceeds current conforming loan limits. For 2009, anything above $417,000 is considered jumbo.

Junior lien A second mortgage or one that subordinates to another loan. Not as common a term as it used to be. You're more likely to hear the terms *second mortgage* or *piggyback*.

Land contract An arrangement where the buyer makes monthly payments to the seller but the ownership of the property does not change hands until the loan is paid in full.

Land-to-value An appraisal term that calculates the value of the land as a percentage of the total value of the home. If the land exceeds the value of the home, it is more difficult to find financing without good comparable sales. Also called lot-to-value.

Lease-purchase agreement Also known as rent-to-own. An option whereby a buyer leases a home until the buyer has saved up enough money for a down payment to qualify for a conventional mortgage.

Lender policy Title insurance that protects a mortgage from defects or previous claims of ownership.

Liability An obligation or bill on the part of the borrower. It works like an automobile loan. When you pay off the car, you get the title. Liabilities such as student loans or a car payment can show up on a credit report, but they can also be anything else that you are obligated to pay. Those liabilities on the credit report are used to determine debt ratios.

LIBOR index *See* London Interbank Offered Rate.

Lien A legal claim or prior interest on the property you're about to buy. Borrowing money from another source in order to buy a house could mean that someone else has a lien on that property.

Loan Money granted to one party with the expectation of it being repaid.

Loan officer The person typically responsible for helping mortgage applicants get qualified and assisting in loan selection and loan application. Loan officers can work at banks, credit unions, and mortgage brokerage houses or for bankers.

Loan processor The person who gathers the required documentation for a loan application for loan submission. Along with your loan officer, you'll work with the loan processor quite a bit during your mortgage process.

Loan underwriter The person responsible for ultimately saying yes or no on a loan file. The underwriter compares loan guidelines with what you have documented in the file.

Loan-to-value ratio LTV is expressed as a percentage of the loan amount when compared to the valuation of the home determined by an appraisal. If a home was appraised at

$100,000 and the loan amount was $70,000, then the LTV would be 70 percent.

Lock An agreement guaranteeing an interest rate over a predetermined period of time. Loan locks are not loan approvals; they're simply the rate your lender has agreed to give you at loan closing.

London Interbank Offered Rate LIBOR is a British index similar to our Federal Funds rate, where British banks borrow money from one another over short periods to adhere to reserve requirements.

LTV See loan-to-value ratio.

Margin A number, expressed as a percentage, that is added to a mortgage's index to determine the rate the borrower pays on the note. An index can be a six-month CD at 4.00 percent and the margin can be 2.00 percent. The interest rate the borrower pays is 4 + 2, or 6.00 percent. A *fully indexed rate* is the index plus the margin.

Market gain The difference between what a mortgage price was when you locked it with the lender and what the mortgage price is when the loan is physically locked with the lender's secondary department or with a mortgage broker's wholesale lender.

Market value In an open market, the market value of a property is both the highest the borrower is willing to pay and the least the seller is willing to accept at the time of contract.

Property appraisals help justify market value by comparing similar home sales in the subject property's neighborhood.

Modifiable mortgage A mortgage loan that allows its interest rate to be modified, even if it's at another lender.

Mortgage A loan with the property being pledged as collateral. The mortgage is retired when the loan is paid in full.

Mortgage-backed securities Investment securities issued by Wall Street firms that are guaranteed, or collateralized, with home mortgages taken out by consumers. These securities can then be bought and sold on Wall Street.

Mortgage bankers Lenders who use their own funds to lend money. Historically, these funds would have come from the savings accounts of other bank customers. But with the evolution of mortgage banking, that's the old way of doing business. Even though bankers use their own money, it may come from other sources, such as lines of credit or through selling loans to other institutions.

Mortgage brokers Companies that set up a home loan between a banker and a borrower. Brokers don't have money to lend directly, but they have experience in finding various loan programs that can suit the borrower, similar to how an independent insurance agent operates. Brokers don't work for the borrower but instead provide mortgage loan choices from other mortgage lenders.

Mortgagee The person or business making the loan; also called the lender.

Mortgage insurance (MI) See private mortgage insurance.

Mortgagor The person(s) getting the loan; also called the borrower.

Multiple Listing Service The MLS is a central repository where real estate brokers and agents show homes and search for homes that are for sale.

Negative amortization A neg-am loan is an adjustable rate mortgage that can have two interest rates, the contract rate or the fully indexed rate. The contract rate is the minimum agreed-on rate the consumer may pay; sometimes the contract rate is lower than the fully indexed rate. The borrower has a choice of which rate to pay, but if the contract rate is lower than the fully indexed rate, that difference is added back to the loan. If your contract payments are only $500 but the fully indexed rate is $700 and you pay only the contract rate, $200 is added back into your original loan amount. Not for the fainthearted, nor for those with little money down.

NINA No income, no asset mortgage. This type of loan does not require that the borrower prove or otherwise document any income or asset whatsoever.

No-fee loan A loan where your lender pays closing costs for you, if you agree to a slightly higher interest rate.

Nonconforming loans Loans whose amounts are above current Fannie or Freddie limits. *See also* jumbo loan.

Note A promise to repay. It may or may not have property involved and may or may not be a mortgage.

Note modification Taking the original terms of a note, and without changing any other part of the obligation or title, reducing the interest rate for the remaining term of the loan. A note modification means you can't shop around for the best rate to reduce your rate; instead, you must work with your original lender who still services your mortgage. In a modification, nothing can change except the rate.

One-time close loan A construction loan whereby you obtain construction financing, permanent financing, and lock in a permanent mortgage rate at the same time. *See also* two-time close loan.

Origination fee A fee charged to cover costs associated with finding, documenting, and preparing a mortgage application, and usually expressed as a percentage of the loan amount.

Owner's policy Title insurance made for the benefit of the homeowner.

Par An interest rate that can be obtained without paying any discount points and that does not have any additional yield beyond its rate. For instance, you get a 30-year quote of 7.00 percent with one point, or 7.25 percent with zero points, or 7.50 percent with zero points plus an additional yield to you of $1,000 toward closing costs. Here the 7.25 percent at zero points is the par rate.

Payment option ARM A type of negative amortization loan where you have a choice as to what you'd like to pay each month. The choice is between an initial contract rate, an interest-only, or a fully indexed, fully amortized loan.

Payment shock A term used by lenders referring to the percentage difference between what you're paying now for housing and what your new payment would be. Most loan programs don't have a payment shock provision, but for those that do, a common percentage increase is 150 percent.

Permanent buydown See buydown.

Piggyback mortgage See second mortgage.

PITI Principal, interest, taxes, and insurance. These figures are used to help determine front debt ratios. In condos, townhouses, or co-ops, HOA dues replace the payment for insurance.

Pledged asset An appraisable property or security that is collateralized to make a mortgage loan. Sometimes a pledged asset can be a stock or mutual fund. A lender can make a mortgage loan and use the mutual fund as part of the collateral. If the borrower fails to make the payments, all or part of the pledged asset can go to the lender.

PMI See private mortgage insurance.

Points See discount points.

Portfolio loan A loan made by a direct lender, usually a bank, and kept in the lender's loan portfolio instead of being sold or underwritten to any external guidelines.

Predatory loan A loan designed to take advantage of people by charging either too many fees or too high of an interest rate, or both, while also stripping those homeowners of their equity.

Prepaid interest Daily interest collected from the day of loan closing to the first of the following month.

Prepayment penalty An amount is paid to the lender if the loan is paid off before its maturity or if extra payments are made on the loan. A *hard penalty* is automatic if the loan is paid off early or if extra payments are made at any time or for any amount whatsoever. A *soft penalty* only lasts for a couple of years and may allow extra payments on the loan not to exceed a certain amount.

Principal The outstanding amount owed on a loan, not including any interest due.

Private mortgage insurance PMI is typically required on all mortgage loans with less than 20 percent down. It is an insurance policy, paid by the borrower with benefits paid to the lender. It covers the difference between the borrower's down payment and 20 percent of the sales price. If the borrower defaults on the mortgage, this difference is paid to the lender.

Pull-through rate A term, used by wholesale lenders, to track the percentage of loans that close that have been locked by a broker.

Quit claim A release of any interest in a property from one party to another. A quit claim does not, however, release the obligation on the mortgage.

Rate-and-term refinance Refinancing to get a new rate. You're changing the interest rate and changing the term, or length, of the new note.

Rate cap How high your ARM rate is permitted to change each adjustment period. There are three possible caps on an adjustable rate mortgage: the adjustment cap, the lifetime rate cap, and the initial rate cap.

Real estate account A mortgage secured by real estate.

Realtor A member of the National Association of Realtors and a registered trademark. Not all real estate agents are Realtors.

Recast A term applied to ARMs and used when extra payments are made to the principal balance. When your note is recast, your monthly payment is calculated for you.

Refinance Obtaining a new mortgage to replace an existing one. There is also a rate-and-term refinance, where only the outstanding principal balance, interest due, and closing costs are included in the loan.

Reissue When refinancing, there may be discounts if you use the same title agency. This "reissue" of an original title report can cost much less than a full title insurance policy.

Rescission Withdrawal from a mortgage agreement. Refinanced mortgage loans for a primary residence have a required three-day "cooling off" period before the loan becomes official. If for any reason you decide not to take the mortgage, you can "rescind" and the whole deal's off.

Reserves A borrower's assets after closing. Reserves can include cash in the bank, stocks, mutual funds, retirement accounts, IRAs, and 401(k) accounts.

Reverse mortgage A mortgage designed to help older Americans who own their homes by paying the homeowner cash in exchange for the equity in their home. When the homeowner no longer owns the home by selling or moving out or dying, then the reverse mortgage lender is paid back all the money borrowed, plus interest.

Revolving account A credit card or department store account on which you typically have a limit and don't make any payments until you charge something.

Sales contract Your written agreement to sell or purchase a home, signed by both the seller and buyer.

Secondary market A financial arena where mortgages are bought and sold, either individually or grouped together into securities backed by those mortgages. Fannie Mae and Freddie Mac are the backbone for the conventional secondary market. Other secondary markets exist for nonconforming loans, subprime loans, and others.

Second mortgage Sometimes called a "piggyback" mortgage, a second mortgage assumes a subordinate position behind a first mortgage. If the home goes into foreclosure, the first mortgage would be settled before the second could lay claim. *See also* junior lien.

Seller The person transferring ownership and all rights to your home in exchange for cash or trade.

Settlement statement Also called the final HUD-1. It shows all financial entries during the home sale, including sales price, closing costs, loan amounts, and property taxes. Your initial good-faith estimate will be your first glimpse of your settlement statement. This statement is one of the final documents put together before you go to closing and is prepared by your attorney or settlement agent.

Subprime loan A loan made to people with less than "prime" credit. There are various stages of subprime credit, from loans for those with simply "tarnished" credit that can't quite get a conventional mortgage, to those with seriously damaged credit who may be in or just out of bankruptcy or have collection accounts or judgments and liens against them.

Survey A map that shows the physical location of the structure and where it sits on the property. A survey also designates any easements that run across or through the property.

Temporary buydown *See* buydown.

Title Legal ownership in a property.

Title exam/title search The process where public records are reviewed to research any previous liens on the property.

Title insurance Protection for the lender, the seller, and/or the borrower against any defects or previous claims to the property being transferred or sold.

Two-time close loan In construction financing, when you first get a construction loan and then get another mortgage at the end of construction. You'll go to two different closings for a two-time close loan. *See also* one-time close loan.

VA loan Government mortgage guaranteed by the Department of Veterans Affairs.

VA no-no A type of VA loan where the borrower not only puts *no* money down, but also pays *no* closing costs.

Verification of deposit A VOD is a form mailed to a bank or credit union that asks the institution to verify that a borrower's bank account exists, how much is in it, how long the borrower has had it, and what the average balance was over the previous two months.

VOD See verification of deposit.

Wraparound mortgage A method of financing where the borrower pays the former owner of the property each month in the form of a mortgage payment. The former owner will then make a mortgage payment to the original mortgage holder.

Index

**Look for These Informative Real Estate Titles at
www.amacombooks.org/go/realestate**

A Survival Guide for Buying a Home, Second Edition by Sid Davis $17.95
A Survival Guide for Selling a Home by Sid Davis $15.00
An Insider's Guide to Refinancing Your Mortgage by David Reed $16.95
Beyond the Bubble by Michael C. Thomsett and Joshua Kahr $16.95
Decoding the New Mortgage Market by David Reed $17.95
Everything You Need to Know Before Buying a Co-op, Condo, or Townhouse by
    Ken Roth $18.95
Financing Your Condo, Co-op, or Townhouse by David Reed $18.95
Home Makeovers That Sell by Sid Davis $15.00
Mortgages 101, Second Edition by David Reed $16.95
Mortgage Confidential by David Reed $16.95
Navigating the Mortgage Minefield by Richard Giannamore and Barbara
    Bardow Osach $17.95
Sell Your Home in Any Market by Jim Remley $15.00
Stop Foreclosure Now by Lloyd Segal $19.95
The First-Time Homeowner's Survival Guide by Sid Davis $16.00
The Home Buyer's Question and Answer Book by Bridget McCrea $16.95
The Landlord's Financial Tool Kit by Michael C. Thomsett $18.95
The Property Management Tool Kit by Mike Beirne $19.95
Untapped Riches by Susan Cutaia, Anthony Cutaia, and Robert Slater $18.95
Who Says You Can't Buy a Home! by David Reed $17.95
Your Eco-Friendly Home by Sid Davis $17.95
Your Guide to VA Loans by David Reed $17.95